MARGARET M. PEARSON

To Harriet and Susannah Cox

Discovering London for Children

Eighth edition

D1387405

SHIRE PUBLICATIONS LTD

Contents

*Copyright © 1983 by Margaret M. Pearson and Shire Publications Ltd.
First published 1971. Revised editions 1972, 1976, 1978, 1980, 1983, 1985.
Eighth edition 1987. ISBN 0 85263 889 2. Number 110 in the Discovering series.*

1. Round and about by bus

More than four thousand of the famous red buses ply up and down streets in London — and out of London — providing transport across some 630 square miles (1630 sq km) within a radius of about 15 miles from Charing Cross.

And if you want to take a comprehensive look at London, to get your bearings and see what you want to explore further, there is no better way than taking an Original London Transport Sightseeing Tour. There are frequent departures from 10 a.m. to 5 p.m. (4 p.m. in winter), then hourly until 8 p.m. every day except Christmas Day, from Grosvenor Gardens near Victoria Station and from Haymarket, Baker Street Station and Marble Arch.

Every bus has an experienced, qualified guide on board to point out the sights and tell you about London. There are some tours with commentaries in French and German.

The tour passes many of London's most famous places, including the Law Courts in Fleet Street, St Paul's Cathedral, the Barbican, the Museum of London, the Monument, London Bridge, Tower Bridge, Westminster Abbey, Horse Guards Parade in Whitehall, Trafalgar Square, Hyde Park Corner and Piccadilly Circus. In the evening many of the buildings are floodlit.

Where to make enquiries

London Regional Transport Travel Information Centres (at Piccadilly Circus, Euston, Victoria, King's Cross, Oxford Circus, Heathrow and St James's Park) supply free information leaflets, including the London Regional Transport Official Tourist Information folded map showing tourist attractions and how to make the most of public transport.

The Travel Information Centres will also sell you tickets offering bargain travel. Long stay visitors can try the 'London Explorer' tickets which give one, three, four or seven days unlimited travel on both buses and Underground within central London and the suburbs (tickets from Travel Information Centres and underground stations). A range of coach tours in and around London is offered throughout the year, from Wilton Road Coach Station, Victoria. You can obtain brochures from Travel Information Centres or National Travel.

3

The red buses (like the Underground) come under the authority of London Regional Transport.

If you have any travel enquiries, telephone 01-222 1234. There is a helpful twenty-four hour service.

Horses to Routemasters

The first regular bus service in London was begun in 1829 by George Shillibeer. His vehicles ran from Paddington Green to the Bank of England, and each was drawn by three horses.

Now, in an average working day, London's red buses carry over 3⅓ million passengers. More than 85 per cent of the services are operated by double-deck vehicles and more than 70 per cent of London buses' scheduled mileage is now run using driver-only buses. Red Arrow buses provide a quick and frequent service in central London, linking the main shopping and entertainment areas with the main line railway stations. Passengers pay a flat rate as they enter and leave through power-operated doors under the control of the driver.

Fifteen hundred double deckers are RMs (Routemasters), seating sixty-four passengers. A longer RM, the RML, seating seventy-two, is also in operation. The 'Metrobus', 'Titan' and 'Olympian' are the latest double deckers, seating sixty-eight to seventy-five passengers, depending on size.

Trafalgar Square is served by more buses than any other place in London. More than 450 buses an hour are scheduled to pass through at peak periods.

London Transport Museum

The London Transport Museum is now housed in the former Flower Market in Covent Garden. Nearly two centuries of London's public transport are represented by historic buses, trams, trolleybuses, locomotives, rolling stock, posters, models, working exhibits and audio-visual displays. The most interesting exhibits include an 1875 knifeboard horse bus, the first omnibus with proper roof seats; a B type motor bus which became the first in the world to be mass-produced; the kind of tram which was in service when the tramways were closed down in 1952; and the world's first underground steam train. Visitors can also operate some exhibits: you can work the driving controls of a 1938 Tube train, a modern bus and an old tram, or even become a modern day signalman operating points and signals in a full-size section of tube tunnel.

Activity sheets for different ages have been designed to encourage observation and deduction, and the musuem's education department arranges special facilties for school parties. At weekends and bank holidays there are film shows and special activities such as model railways in action.

Admission
Daily except Christmas Day and Boxing Day, from 10 a.m. to 6 p.m., last entry at 5.15 p.m. There is a coffee bar and a well-stocked museum shop. For further information telephone 01-379 6344. Admission charge.

How to get there
Covent Garden, Leicester Square or Charing Cross Underground stations; or by bus to the Strand or Aldwych.

2. The Underground

Beneath London and its suburbs runs one of the largest electric underground systems in the world. It goes in all directions, and covers such a wide area that when the outskirts are reached, it comes up to ground level and operates as an ordinary surface railway. From Mondays to Fridays more than 2 million passenger journeys are made daily on this vast system, popularly known as the Underground.

There are basically two types of tunnels: 'cut and cover', constructed by digging a deep trench for the railway and then covering it over, and 'tube', constructed by boring through the ground from underground working sites. 254 route miles are run by the Underground; 105 of these are in tunnel—85 in 'tube' and 20 in 'cut and cover'.

The first sub-surface steam railway, which was nearly four miles long, was opened in 1863 and ran between Paddington and Farringdon Street. The newest complete Underground 'line' is the Victoria Line, which links Brixton, Victoria and the West End with the main railway stations at Euston, King's Cross and St Pancras, and with the densely populated north-eastern suburbs. This was opened by the Queen in 1969. The extension of the Piccadilly Line to Heathrow Central opened in 1977 and the Jubilee Line link between Baker Street and Charing Cross was opened by the Prince of Wales in 1979.

Facts and curiosities

Escalators capable of carrying nine thousand passengers an hour in either direction at speeds of 90 to 145 feet (27 to 44m) per minute are installed at seventy stations. The longest escalator is at Leicester Square—161 feet 6 inches (49.2 m) on a slope with a vertical rise of 80 feet 9 inches (24.6 m). The station with the most escalators is Oxford Circus, with fourteen.

In Bayswater, at 23 and 24 Leinster Gardens, dummy housefronts were built to preserve the street frontage when the Circle Line was cut close to the road.

A river flows above the platforms of Sloane Square underground station. An iron aqueduct carries the Westbourne, which flows from Hampstead to the Thames, via the Serpentine.

The busiest underground stations are Victoria, Oxford Circus, King's Cross, Piccadilly Circus, Waterloo and Liverpool Street.

The best way to explore London is on foot and several organisations arrange guided walks through historic London. The walks usually start outside an underground station. You pay a fee to join the party and the walk takes a couple of hours. Most take place at weekends and the London Tourist Board (01-730 3488) will give you details.

3. Round trip on the river

Frequent trips run from Westminster Pier both up and down the river. Some of the launches go up river as far as Hampton Court during the summer, and as far down river as Greenwich, where the *Cutty Sark* and *Gipsy Moth IV* are in permanent dry dock, or Woolwich, where the Thames Barrier is. Perhaps the most popular river excursion is a round trip from Westminster Pier down to Tower Bridge and back; a trip taking well under an hour.

Why 'Big Ben'?

Westminster Pier is reached by steps leading down to the quay from near the bronze statue of Boadicea in her chariot, near Big Ben and at the end of Westminster Bridge (which was built about one hundred years ago).

Big Ben, by the way, is a bell, not a clock, though the clock, the chimes and even the tower itself are affectionately, if incorrectly, all thought of as Big Ben. It may have been called Big Ben after Sir Benjamin Hall, then First Commissioner of Works, or after a popular prize fighter, Benjamin Caunt. They were both 'big' enough; they each weighed 17 stone (108 kg). Big Ben itself was cast at the Whitechapel Foundry in 1858. It has been in the belfry ever since. Each of the four faces of the clock is 23 feet (39.9 m) in diameter, and even the minute spaces are a foot (0.3 m) square.

As you head by boat towards Tower Bridge, old **Scotland Yard** is on the left, in red brick and Portland stone. (In 1967, Scotland Yard moved to a huge new building in Broadway, off Victoria Street.)

Straight ahead is **Hungerford Bridge,** which carries the main railway line across the river from Charing Cross Station. It is not a glamorous bridge, and the foot bridge is definitely unattractive, but it gives a wonderful view, particularly at night, of St Paul's, the Royal Festival Hall, and the lights of London reflected in the dark water.

Next landmark on the left is the obelisk **Cleopatra's Needle,** round which Moses is said to have played as a boy. Behind the Embankment Gardens is Shell-Mex House and the Savoy Hotel.

The next bridge is **Waterloo Bridge,** the second of its name, and well worth walking across one day to see the fine view both upstream and down (and the swans paddling about on the muddy banks when the tide is out).

'Somerset had his head cut off'

Then comes the famous **Somerset House,** with its 600 foot (183 m) facade facing the Thames. It was for many years the home of the Registry of Births, Marriages and Deaths; and here wills were deposited, among them those of Shakespeare, Van Dyck, Isaac Newton and John Milton. (The Registry is now at St Catherine's House, Aldwych.) The building occupies the site of the princely palace begun by Edward Seymour, Lord Protector Somerset, uncle of the child-king Edward VI, whose mother Jane Seymour (third wife of Henry VIII) died shortly after his birth. Somerset was one of the regents appointed to rule England during Edward's minority, but he was outwitted by more ruthless rivals and executed in 1522, wearing for the occasion a splendid costume fine enough for a State banquet. (The unfeeling young king, to whom his uncle had always been kind, entered in his journal the terse comment: 'Somerset had his head cut off'.) Elizabeth lived for a time at Somerset House while her sister was on the throne, and Oliver Cromwell lay in state there for five weeks while preparations were made for his funeral.

Moored by the Embankment near Somerset House and the Temple Gardens are a river police station; the *Wellington,* which serves as the Livery Hall of the Master Mariners' Company; and two training ships used by the London Division of the Royal

7

Naval Volunteer Reserve — HMS *Chrysanthemum* and *President.*

On the opposite bank stands the spacious arts complex, containing the **National Theatre,** National Film Theatre and Hayward Gallery. The tiers of concrete architecture provide a good contrast to the more ornate and historical buildings on the river.

The tallest Wren steeple

Just before reaching **Blackfriars Bridge** you can glimpse the three-tiered 'wedding cake' spire of **St Bride's Church,** the tallest of all Wren's steeples. Samuel Pepys was born nearby and was christened in the old church, where Richard Lovelace, the Cavalier poet, was buried. It was Lovelace who wrote the famous lines: *Stone walls do not a prison make, Nor iron bars a cage.*

Blackfriars Bridge takes its name from the black habits of the Dominican friars whose priory backed on to the Thames. Their Great Hall was the scene of the trial of Catharine of Aragon (held before Cardinal Wolsey) when Henry VIII was seeking a divorce in order to marry Anne Boleyn.

Away on the left is **St Paul's Cathedral,** and just before Southwark Bridge you can see the spire of another Wren church—**St James Garlickhithe.** The derivation of this word is interesting. It was a district where many Italians settled, who ate and sold garlic.

Old London Bridge

After passing under Southwark Bridge and Cannon Street Railway Bridge, we come to **London Bridge,** which thousands of people cross every day, flooding the City with workers in the morning, and draining it almost empty as they leave in the evening. The famous Old London Bridge stood a few hundred yards to the east of the present bridge. There were various early wooden bridges over the river, but the most famous bridge of all was the stone bridge built by Peter, Chaplain of St Mary Colechurch; not so unlikely a man as might be supposed, as the church had from early days encouraged bridge building as an act of piety. The stone for Peter's bridge was mainly Kentish rag. It was begun in 1176, finished in 1209, and remained the *only* bridge over the tidal Thames till 1739. It stood on nineteen great supports with a spiked drawbridge in the southern half. The heads (and sometimes the quarters) of executed people were often stuck on the spikes till they rotted and fell off. Houses, shops and a chapel (to St Thomas à Becket) were built on the bridge, the rents from the houses and shops going towards the cost of the upkeep. This wonderful old bridge was finally demolished—with much regret on all sides—only after the completion of John Rennie's bridge in 1831.

Rennie's bridge has now been demolished piecemeal, and rebuilt at the same time. This work was begun at the end of 1967. The new bridge carries six lanes of traffic. Rennie's bridge has been reconstructed in Arizona, USA.

That part of the Thames that is downstream from London Bridge is called the Port of London, upstream is the King's Reach, while immediately downstream is the famous Pool of London.

Just past London Bridge you will see the top of **The Monument** and **Billingsgate,** which was once London's big fish market. Billingsgate Wharf is probably the oldest on the river; it had been used by fishermen ever since the ninth century before the market was moved. Billingsgate takes its name from an old gate called after Belin, a legendary king of the Britons. It claimed to be the only market in the world where every kind of fish was sold—'wet, dry and shell'.

Traitor's Gate

Next comes the church of **All Hallows by-the-Tower** and then we pass the **Tower of London** (and the Traitor's Gate) with **HMS Belfast** moored opposite, and finally reach **Tower Bridge,** the most famous and picturesque bridge across the Thames today. The 800 foot (244 metre) span between the Gothic towers of the bridge can be raised in two parts to let ships pass up and down the river. The two drawbridges weigh 1,000 tonnes each, but they can be raised (by hydraulic machinery) in 1½ minutes. The towers are now open to the public.

Going back towards Westminster Pier we pass on the left warehouses and wharves. At the southern end of London Bridge is **Southwark Cathedral,** a much-restored medieval church—possibly the finest Gothic building in London after Westminster Abbey. There is a chapel in the cathedral called after John Harvard, founder of Harvard University in Massachusetts in the United States. He was the son of a Southwark butcher and was christened in the church in 1607. Shakespeare's younger brother, Edmund, who died the same year, is buried in the cathedral. Southwark is a district Shakespeare knew well. The Globe Theatre was built by his friends the Burbages in 1599, and he acted there and had fifteen of his plays produced there.

Someone on the launch will probably point out a seventeenth century house from which Sir Christopher Wren is said to have watched the building of St Paul's (which is almost directly opposite). But there is no evidence that Wren ever lived there, or that he annoyed his wife by rushing to the window without even waiting to put on his wig!

Festival Hall and County Hall

Under Blackfriars and Waterloo Bridges again, and on the left is the **Royal Festival Hall,** whose auditorium seats three thousand. At the back you can see the two big blocks of the **Shell Centre** (linked by a tunnel). The blocks cover 7½ acres (3 ha). They were completed in 1962. The last big building before returning to Westminster Pier is **County Hall,** 750 feet (229 m) long, for many years the headquarters first of the London County Council and then the Greater London Council.

In the summer, all along the river front by the Festival Hall, there is a lively market every Saturday and Sunday. Sometimes tents are erected; sometimes plain stalls. They sell fashion-wear, jewellery and both second hand and new books.

As the launch turns you can see **St Thomas's Hospital** on the left, and directly opposite the **Houses of Parliament,** which incorporate the magnificent old Westminster Hall. The tallest tower is the Victoria Tower, 336 feet (102 m) high and 75 feet (22.8 m) square—the tallest square tower in the world. A flag flies from this tower during the day if Parliament is sitting. If it is sitting at night, a light shines in the Clock Tower.

During the summer only, you can telephone Westminster Pier and enquire about the trips from 01-930 4097. Or ask about river trips (and other excursions) at the London Visitor and Convention Bureau (01-730 3488), which has information centres at Victoria Station, Selfridges, Harrods, Heathrow Central Station and, in summer, at the Tower of London.

4. Westminster Abbey

Westminster Abbey is such an enormous place (550 feet, 167 m long), with so much to see, that it is easiest to explore if you divide it into three—Edward the Confessor's Chapel, Henry VII's Chapel, and the Abbey of the 'commoners'.

The 'commoners' Abbey is itself divided (very roughly) into different areas for different types of people. Poets and writers tend to be buried or commemorated near Chaucer in Poets' Corner in the South Transept (on the right of the nave); statesmen round William Pitt and Gladstone in the North Transept; musicians around Henry Purcell in the north aisle of the Choir, and scientists around Sir Isaac Newton near the Choir Screen.

Prime interest in the Abbey is always centred on Edward the Confessor's Chapel, commemorating the founder of the church, and in Henry VII's magnificent chapel where he and his wife are buried together with other sovereigns who came after him. There is an admission charge for the royal chapels, transepts and Choir. Last tickets sold, Monday to Friday, 4 p.m. and Saturday

2 p.m. (although the Abbey sometimes reopens at 3.45 p.m.). It opens on Wednesday evenings 6 p.m. to 7.45 p.m.

The first Norman building in England

When London was the chief town of the small kingdom of Essex, King Sebert of Essex built the first church of St Peter on Thorney Island, a marshy island formed by two streams flowing into the Thames.

This building was largely destroyed by the Danes, and **Edward the Confessor,** who had a special affection for St Peter, founded the church, later rebuilt by Henry III. Its official name is now 'the Collegiate Church of St Peter in Westminster'.

Edward, with his brilliant eyes and long white hair, was much revered by his subjects. His abbey church was almost as large as the present building, except for Henry VII's Chapel. Edward had been brought up in Normandy and was fond of both that country and its people, so the church, under his guidance, became the first Norman structure in England. It was finished at Christmas time, 1065.

In the first week of 1066 Edward died and was buried in the Abbey. King Harold was killed at Hastings, and on Christmas Day **William The Conqueror** was crowned in the Abbey. William, like Edward, created a precedent—Edward by being buried in the Abbey, William by being crowned there. Up to the time of George II, all but a handful of our sovereigns were buried in the Abbey, and all but two—Edward V and Edward VIII—have been crowned there. William is not buried in the Abbey, but perhaps King Sebert is. The tomb thought to be his is by the gates of the South Ambulatory.

The king who closed the shops of London

Edward the Confessor's church was very largely rebuilt by Henry III (King John's son), who wanted to honour the memory and the remains of the saintly Edward. **Henry III** (1216-1272) was a pious spendthrift. He had a genuine appreciation for art, and wanted to build something for London that would rival the beauties of Rheims and Amiens. He raised the money in various ways. Having 'persuaded' a Jewish widow to present £2,500 to his rebuilding fund, he impulsively had all his children weighed—and their weight in gold given to the the poor. He instituted a fair in Tothill Fields near Westminster Abbey to raise money for his project and commanded all shops in London to close for fifteen days, so that the fair would make more money for the building fund. (But it rained and rained, and the people in London suffered 'pitifullie in mire and durt'.) He got into such financial difficulties that he and his wife, Eleanor of Provence, had to invite themselves out to dine with London's wealthy merchants. In 1267, he pawned the jewels he had collected for Edward the Confessor's shrine. However, he promised to restore them within eighteen months — and he did. He was so pious that during a visit to France he insisted on saying a mass at every church he passed. This so annoyed the French king that he ordered every church on the way to Paris to close as the royal procession approached.

In 1269, the new building was consecrated, and Edward the Confessor's body was placed in the magnificent new shrine.

EDWARD THE CONFESSOR'S CHAPEL

As time went by, other kings and queens were buried around the Confessor's shrine — (from the right as you walk round) Queen Eleanor (wife of Edward I), Henry III, Edward I, Richard II and his queen, Anne of Bohemia, Edward III and his queen, Philippa of Hainault. Henry V is buried beneath his own Chantry Chapel to the east of the Confessor's shrine.

Henry III died in 1272, and was buried in a splendid tomb, once studded with jewels and glass mosaic. But his heart (as he had promised) was sent to the Abbey of Fontevrault in France, where Richard Coeur de Lion and his grandfather Henry II were buried.

An heroic queen and a boy king who lost his slipper

Queen Eleanor of Castile died in 1290. She had been Edward I's constant companion throughout their married life, even accompanying him on Crusades. She was a greatly loved woman, for her courage in sucking poison from a wound when Edward was attacked by an assassin in the Holy Land, for her kindness to the poor, and for her loving care of her seven surviving daughters and one surviving son. An anniversary memorial service was held at her tomb for at least 250 years, with one hundred candles burning and all the bells clanging.

Queen Philippa of Hainault and her husband **Edward III** (died 1377) were the parents of twelve children, including the Black Prince. **Richard II** was the son of the Black Prince. Richard, who was only ten when he succeeded his grandfather, fainted during the long Coronation service. Knights cleared a way for him, and as he was carried out of the Abbey to the Palace of Westminster, through the surging crowd, he lost 'one of the blessed slippers of the regalia'. When he grew up, Richard replaced the lost slipper with a pair of velvet shoes. Richard's **Queen Anne** (of Bohemia) died of the plague. He was later murdered at Pontefract Castle, and buried obscurely at King's Langley. Henry V had his body exhumed to give it a more seemly burial. He adorned the corpse with royal robes, and himself followed Richard's second funeral as chief mourner. This time Richard was buried in the Abbey, and now shares a double tomb with his much-loved Anne.

Three chargers at the high altar

Henry V, a popular hero after the battle of Agincourt, and a generous benefactor to the Abbey, was given one of the most impressive funerals the Abbey has ever witnessed. The king died in 1422 (probably of dysentery) aged thirty-three, while campaigning in France. His black-hung, sombre funeral procession wound its way some 250 miles from Vincennes to Paris, across the Channel from Calais to Dover, and up to London where the body of the dead king was met by all the bishops in England. Clergy chanted unceasingly as they followed with 1,400 lighted tapers. Behind the bier came Henry's attractive young wife, Catherine de Valois. When the procession reached the Abbey, Henry's three chargers were led right up to the High Altar. They carried his armour. His helmet, saddle and shield are now on view in the Exhibition of Treasures. The effigy on his tomb had been carved in his own lifetime of solid oak, with his head and hands made of silver. In Henry VIII's reign the silver was stolen and Henry V was headless till 1971 when he was given a head and hands of polyester resin.

Pepys visits royalty

When **Catharine de Valois** (the wife of Henry V and Owen Tudor) died in 1437, she was buried with great pomp in the Lady Chapel. Henry VII pulled this chapel down when building his own, and Catharine's body was eventually placed in a coffin of loose boards by Henry V's tomb. The vergers of the day for a shilling a time would take off the lid to allow visitors to see the royal remains. Samuel Pepys went one better. In 1669, he wrote that he saw... 'the body of Queen Catharine of Valois, and I had the upper part of her body in my hands, and I did kiss her mouth, reflecting upon it that I did kiss a Queene, and that this was my birthday thirty-six years old that I did kiss a Queene'. Catharine was finally buried under the altar slab in Henry V's Chantry Chapel.

The Coronation Chair

At the far end of the Confessor's Chapel is the somewhat battered Coronation Chair, made for Edward I. Under its seat is the famous Stone of Scone, upon which Scottish kings were crowned for hundreds of years. Edward brought it to London after he had defeated the Scots in 1296. For Coronation

13

ceremonies, the chair is placed in the Sanctuary (the space between the altar rails). The only times the chair has left the Abbey were when Cromwell had it taken to Westminster Hall for his installation as Lord Protector, and when it was taken away for safety during the two World Wars.

HENRY VII'S CHAPEL

The main part of the Abbey as we know it was the work of Henry III, carried out during twenty-five years, but the completed church is the work of various kings (and abbots) over five centuries.

Henry VII was the other great royal builder. His magnificent chapel, one of the glories of England, completely transformed the eastern end of the Abbey. The handsome gates to the chapel are of oak and bronze, divided into open panels, and decorated with heraldic devices to commemorate the fact that the marriage of Henry VII (a Lancastrian) to Elizabeth (of York) finally ended the War of the Roses. The falcon represents Elizabeth's father, Edward IV, the daisy and portcullis make a punning reference to Henry's mother, Margaret Beaufort, the leopards represent England, and a crown and double roses on a thorn bush recall Henry's own hasty first coronation on the battlefield when Richard III was killed at Bosworth.

These gates lead to the double row of seats for the Knights of the Bath, which run along both sides of the nave of the chapel. Each stall has a tip-up seat, carved with strange creatures — pigs and dragons, a mermaid and her comb, a jester, three monkeys and a cooking pot, and the devil himself, playing a drum.

Sixty kings, queens, princes and princesses

In Henry VII's Chapel some sixty kings and queens, princes and princesses lie under the bright silk banners of the Knights of the Bath and under the delicate fan tracery of the exquisite roof. Henry himself died in 1509, about ten years before the building was completed. He was buried where he had planned to be buried, with his wife. Their tomb is shared by **James I** (died 1625), who has no memorial. Under the altar lies the young Tudor king, **Edward VI,** who died of consumption at the age of fifteen in 1553.

Two sisters and 'the little princes in the Tower'

There are two important chapels in the North and South Aisles of Henry VII's Chapel. The entrances are clearly marked on either side of the gates.

The North Aisle is the **Queen Elizabeth Chapel.** Here the coffin of the great Tudor queen (died 1603) lies on top of that of her half-sister, 'Bloody' Mary (died 1558). **Mary** had no memorial at all till James I had a Latin epitaph inscribed on the tomb: *Consorts both in throne and grave, here rest two sisters, in the hope of one resurrection.*

This chapel has sometimes been called the Chapel of the Innocents. In it are buried the 'little princes in the Tower' — twelve-year-old **Edward V** and his ten-year-old brother Richard, murdered together in 1483. The urn was designed by Christopher Wren at the request of Charles II. Here, too, lie two little daughters of James I — the baby Princess Sophia in her coloured alabaster cradle and coverlet (one of the most charming memorials to be seen anywhere) and, in stomacher and Medici collar, her two-year-old sister Mary. Watched over by her nurses, the little girl murmured 'I go...I go...Away I go!'

Mary, Queen of Scots, and Queen Anne's eighteen children

Opposite Queen Elizabeth's Chapel in the South Aisle is the Lady Margaret Chapel, where **Margaret Beaufort, Countess of Richmond,** Mother of Henry VII, is buried, in one of the most beautiful of all the Abbey monuments. She was the founder of Christ's and St John's Colleges, Cambridge.

In the same chapel is a memorial to **Margaret Douglas, Countess of Lennox,** the mother of Lord Darnley, whose marriage to Mary, Queen of Scots, proved so disastrous. (She was thus the grandmother of James VI of Scotland — James I of England.)

Mary, Queen of Scots, lies in a fine tomb decorated with Scottish thistles. After her execution in 1587 she was buried in Peterborough Cathedral, but twenty-five years later her son James I had her reburied in the Abbey.

In this aisle also are buried **Charles II** (died 1685) and **William and Mary** (William died in 1702, following an accident when his horse stumbled over a molehill; Mary died in 1694).

Queen Anne (died 1714) and her husband are also buried in the Lady Margaret Chapel with their eighteen children. One boy lived to be ten. The others were all stillborn or died in infancy.

The Battle of Britain

Henry VII's Chapel was the last of the royal additions and alterations to the Abbey, but the very end of the chapel — the east end of the Abbey — has been made into a special RAF Battle of Britain Remembrance Chapel.

The windows here contain the badges of sixty-three Fighter Squadrons which took part in the Battle of Britain, and above the badges are the flags of the Dominions and Allies whose men were amongst those killed. At the foot of the windows are Shakespeare's words, spoken by Henry V: *We few, we happy few, we band of brothers.*

15

THE COMMONERS' ABBEY

Churchill

Having explored Edward the Confessor's Shrine and Henry VII's Chapel, there is still the rest of the Abbey to be seen.

Only a few steps inside the West Door is a green marble slab saying simply: *Remember Winston Churchill. In accordance with the wishes of the Queen and Parliament, the Dean and Chapter placed this stone on the twenty fifth anniversary of the Battle of Britain, 15th September, 1965.*

Churchill spoke of the valiant, outnumbered Battle of Britain fighter pilots the famous words: 'Never in the field of human conflict was so much owed by so many to so few'. He died in 1965, and is buried in the country churchyard of Bladon, near Blenheim Palace, in Oxfordshire, where he was born.

A body picked at random

A few steps further on is the grave of **the Unknown Warrior.**

The idea of burying an unknown soldier was suggested by the Reverend David Railton, MC, a chaplain in the First World War. He saw a grave in France with the pencilled inscription: 'An unknown soldier of the Black Watch'. The British government approved the idea. The bodies of four men killed in the main battle areas of France — the Aisne, the Somme, Arras and Ypres — were placed in a chapel. Each man was covered with a Union Jack, and one was picked at random by the general officer in charge of troops in France and Flanders. He was brought to England and given the funeral of a king on Armistice Day, 11th November, 1920. The procession was headed by King George V, and as the coffin reached the Abbey, it passed through two lines of holders of the Victoria Cross. The body was buried in earth brought from France under a marble slab quarried in Belgium. Nearby, on a pillar, hangs the American Congressional Medal, bestowed on the Unknown Warrior by the government of the United States of America.

Murdered for his ring

Tombs and memorials are thick along the walls of the Abbey. Many of the people honoured are now forgotten, but sometimes men who are at least half-forgotten come into the news again.

One such man is **Admiral Sir Cloudesley Shovel,** whose tomb is in the South Aisle (which leads to Poets' Corner). Until a few

16

years ago most people would have passed his monument without a second glance. But in 1968 and 1969, divers off the Isles of Scilly discovered the wreck of the *Association* and other ships that foundered there in 1707 when returning to England after a battle with the French. The ships lost their bearings in bad weather, and the *Association,* carrying Shovel's flag, struck the Western Rocks, and broke up. Shovel was washed ashore but was murdered by a woman for a ring he was wearing.

The poet who was buried standing up

Poets' Corner was first mentioned as such by Oliver Goldsmith (who is remembered here but is buried in the Temple churchyard). The principal tomb (against the wall on the right) is that of **Geoffrey Chaucer** (died 1400), author of *The Canterbury Tales.* Also buried in Poets' Corner are Edmund Spenser (died 1599), author of *The Faerie Queene,* Charles Dickens, Tennyson, Browning, Hardy and Kipling. There are memorials to Longfellow, as a tribute to American poetry, to the Brontë sisters, to Shakespeare, Keats, Shelley, Robert Burns and John Milton. **Ben Jonson** (died 1637) comes off best. He has a memorial in Poets' Corner — and is buried in the Nave. There are various stories about Jonson, who was born in the neighbourhood and educated at Westminster School. He was a friend of Shakespeare and tutor to Sir Walter Raleigh's son. He is said to have asked Charles I a favour — for 18 square inches of ground. 'Where?' asked the king. 'In Westminster Abbey!' came the answer — and he was buried in the Abbey, standing up. (Nearby is **David Livingstone,** the African explorer and missionary, who is buried under a large grey slab let into the stone in the centre of the Nave. He died in the middle of Africa in 1873.)

He lived for 150 years

History seems eternal when you go through the Abbey. So does life itself if you look at a small memorial in the floor in Poets' Corner — to **Thomas Parr,** a Shropshire farm servant. He lived on and on, remarried at 120, had a child, and finally called it quits when he was 150. He lived from 1485 to 1635 — through the reigns of Richard III, Henry VII, Henry VIII and his three children Edward VI, Mary and Elizabeth, James I and Charles I, who entertained him so royally that perhaps he helped the old man on his way to Paradise!

Dick Whittington and his cat

Very little of the ancient glass is left in Westminster Abbey. Some was deliberately destroyed by the Puritans, some was broken during rebuilding and restoration work, and some was destroyed during the Second World War. But on the north side

17

of the Nave (on the left as you enter by the West Door) is a series of windows designed and carried out by Sir Ninian Comper, RA, between 1907 and 1961. Each window embodies figures of the kings and abbots in whose reigns the Abbey was gradually built — and incorporates legends or incidents connected with them.

Thus Edward the Confessor is shown with the Charter of the Foundation of the Abbey, and he is holding up the ring which, according to legend, he gave to St John the Evangelist, who appeared to him disguised as a beggar. Other kings shown in these windows are Henry III, Henry V (with a small picture at the bottom left-hand corner of his great Mayor of London — Dick Whittington — and his cat, a marmalade one), Richard II, Edward III and Edward I. A scene in this window shows Henry III's heart being handed over to the abbess of Fontevrault.

The 'flogging headmaster'

The black and white pavement in the Choir was presented by **Dr Richard Busby,** the 'flogging headmaster' of Westminster School both during the Commonwealth (though he made no secret of his royalist sympathies) and after the Restoration. In spite of his respect for royalty, he refused to remove his cap in the presence of Charles II. 'If I did,' he said, 'the boys would think you more important than I'. He died in 1695 and is buried beneath his black and white pavement.

5. Westminster Abbey Museum

We have read in the previous chapter that for over nine hundred years sovereigns have been crowned and buried in Westminster Abbey. It was once the custom to place life-sized effigies of sovereigns and other famous people on their coffins at their funerals. After the funeral, the effigy would lie in state, and some were eventually stored in Henry V's Chantry.

Many of the Westminster Abbey effigies have just crumbled away and been lost, but a dozen or so are on show in the Westminster Abbey Museum in the beautiful Norman Undercroft in the Cloisters. The oldest are of wood, hay and plaster. Later ones were made of wax. There are other sections of this compact museum which show how the Abbey developed and how it, the effigies and other treasures fit into the history of the country. The apparently magnificent 'Crown Jewels' on display are the reproductions used at coronation rehearsals in the Abbey before the great day. Some of the regalia, though, belongs to the Abbey and the superb gold-thread Cope was used at the Coronation of Charles II in 1661.

A left-handed king

The oldest funeral effigy in Europe is that of **Edward III,** the victor of Crecy. His face, of wood, shows his mouth and left-hand cheek affected by the stroke that killed him in 1377. Doctors who examined the effigy when it was restored some years ago decided that Edward was left-handed. He was, nevertheless, noted for his fine penmanship. Edward was a handsome man, and during restoration, some of his hair was found — still reddish-gold. (The hair was analysed by forensic laboratory experts at Scotland Yard. They found that the effigy's eyebrows were made of dog's hair!)

Anne of Bohemia died of the plague in 1394, leaving her king Richard II disconsolate. (For a year after her death he refused to enter any door they had entered together.) Though the head of Anne's funeral effigy is of oak, it was carved form a death mask attributed to one Roger Elys, a tallow chandler in London, noted for his waxworks at the end of the fourteenth century. Some of Anne's hair was caught in a nail driven into the oaken head. It was brown.

The sword of Henry V

Another fine effigy is that of **Catharine de Valois,** the attractive wife of Henry V, and later of Owen Tudor, founder of the great Tudor dynasty. There is a special display of the funeral armour of Henry V, including what is probably the oldest saddle in Europe.

The most striking exhibit is the death mask of **Henry VII.** This mask (made in 1509) reveals every detail of his bone structure and features — the determined, slightly humorous mouth, the firm nose and observant eyes. Small tufts of hair, red turning to grey, have been found round the ears.

The playing-card queen

The effigy of Henry's queen, **Elizabeth of York,** shows a broad, well-covered face. Said to be the queen in all four suits of playing cards made in England, she died in 1503. She was related to no fewer than ten kings and queens — Edward IV (father), Edward V (brother), Richard III (uncle), Henry VII (husband), Henry VIII (son), and Edward VI (grandson). Mary Tudor and Elizabeth I were both her granddaughters, and her own daughters both married kings — Margaret becoming the wife of James IV of Scotland, and Mary marrying Louis XII of France.

A curiosity among the effigies is that of **General Monk,** a leader in the Cromwellian Army who was largely responsible for the restoration of Charles II. Monk's effigy is encased in full armour and wears a fresh white neckerchief.

The most famous of the effigies is that of **Charles II** — 'a tall dark man, above two yards high' (as he was described in a proclamation offering £1,000 for his betrayal after his escape from the battle of Worcester). The effigy is dressed in his own garter robes and cloth-of-silver doublet and breeches. He died in 1685, asking as he lay dying: 'Open the curtains, that I may once more see the day'.

The oldest stuffed bird in England

Frances Stuart, later the **Duchess of Richmond and Lennox,** was one of the many women whom Charles II admired. She was generally considered a great beauty, and posed for the figure of Britannia on our old pennies. She died in 1702. Her little parrot, a favourite pet, died a few days later. It is exhibited with her — the oldest stuffed bird in England.

Catherine, Duchess of Buckingham (died 1743), is also here in effigy. She was the illegitimate daughter of James II by Catherine Sedley. James loved her deeply, but she said: 'It cannot be for my beauty, because I haven't any, and it cannot be for my wit, because he hasn't enough to know I have any'. The duchess, however, had little sense of humour, and took her royal blood very seriously, insisting that visitors should bow themselves out backwards. John Sheffield, first Duke of Buckingham (the Lord Chamberlain), was her second husband. He built the original house where Buckingham Palace now stands.

As well as effigies, there are several commemorative figures in the Museum. The most striking of these is **Lord Nelson,** who died at the battle of Trafalgar in 1805. He was buried in St Paul's. This excellent model is dressed in his own clothes. Gieves, the tailor who made his uniform, and Lock's of St James's, who made his cocked hat (with a green shade attached to cover his blind eye), are still in business in London.

Gift from a queen

The most romantic exhibit in the Museum is the gold and cameo ring Elizabeth I gave to her young favourite, **Robert Devereux, Earl of Essex,** telling him to send it to her if ever he were in peril. The time came when he was in deadly peril — under sentence of death in the Tower of London. He sent the ring to the queen, but court jealousy prevented it reaching her, and Essex was executed in 1601. This ring was once set (under glass) into Elizabeth's tomb in the Abbey, but after an attempt was made to prise it out of its setting in 1964, it was put into the

Abbey's museum for safe keeping.

Admission
   The museum is open every day except Sunday, 10.30 a.m. to 4 p.m. There is an admission charge.

6. Trooping the Colour and Changing the Guard

Trooping the Colour is a military ceremony held on the sovereign's official birthday, which is always on a Saturday in June. It begins at 11 a.m. Two rehearsals are held on the previous two Saturdays and the ceremony itself will be postponed if the weather is too bad. The Guards' uniforms are so expensive they must not be allowed to become soaked.
   'Colours' are ceremonial silk flags: consecrated symbolic emblems of a regiment's or battalion's traditions. They are held in high esteem and treated with great respect, always being carried by officers and guarded by colour-sergeants. Trooping the Colour originated in an old ceremony known as lodging the colour. This was performed at the end of the day and no soldier was allowed to dismiss until the colour had been lodged in the billet of the officer in charge of it.
   In the expression Trooping the Colour, the word 'trooping' means marching to music, and the drill of the Guards performing the Trooping the Colour has made the ceremony world famous, and you must get to the Horse Guards Parade early if you are to have a chance of seeing it.
   The ceremony is both long and complicated. Only after the men have fallen in under their officers is the colour handed over by the Regimental Sergeant-Major to the Ensign of the Escort. Then comes the actual trooping, when the colour is marched along the ranks so that every man can see it and recognise it. (This was a matter of great importance when colours were carried in battle, as the flags were rallying points for soldiers.)
   The trooping is followed by the famous march past, in both slow and quick time, to the music of massed bands. The Queen takes the salute and then returns to Buckingham Palace in a carriage at the head of her Guards.
   The scarlet tunics and bearskins are common to the Brigade of Guards as a whole.

21

Each regiment has distinguishing features of uniform:

Regiment	Hatband	Bearskin	Buttons
Grenadier	Scarlet	White goat-hair plume on left	Set singly
Coldstream	White	Scarlet plume on right	Set in pairs
Scots	Red, white and green diced	No plume	Set in threes
Irish	Green	Pale blue feather plume on right	Set in fours
Welsh	Black	White and green plume on left	Set in fives

Admission

Seating for both the rehearsals and the actual Trooping is balloted for, and applications for tickets (two only for each applicant) must be made to the Brigade Major, Household Division, Horse Guards, Whitehall, London SW1, before 1st March each year. Be sure to enclose a stamped addressed envelope. Tickets for the first reheasal are free. There is a charge for tickets for the second rehearsal and for the Trooping itself (telephone 01-930 4466 for current prices) with no reduction for children. Standing room is free down the approach road, but it is a question of arriving early enough to see what is going on. There is always a huge crowd.

The Changing of the Guard

Horse Guards Parade, where the Trooping is held, is on the site of the old tilt-yard of Whitehall Palace. An archway leads from the parade ground to the courtyard where mounted sentries of the Queen's Life Guard are relieved every hour — and where the Changing of the Guard takes place every day at 11 a.m. (except on Sundays, when it is held at 10 a.m.). The ceremony takes about half an hour. It is colourful and photogenic, so there is always a crowd in the very limited space. The Queen's Life Guard, mounted on black horses, is provided by the Household Cavalry.

Everyone may *walk* through the archway — but only the Queen and a very few privileged people are allowed to *drive* through.

There is another Guard changing ceremony, that of the Queen's Guard at Buckingham Palace where, daily from April to early autumn, every other day during the winter months, the Guard is changed in the yard in front of the palace. The new guard marches behind a band from Wellington Barracks and arrives in the forecourt at about 11.30 a.m. This ceremony also lasts about half an hour. When the Court is in London, the Queen's Colour of crimson is carried. Otherwise the Regimental Colour, based on the Union Jack, is carried. In very bad weather, the formal ceremony is cancelled.

How to get there
Horse Guards Parade is a few minutes' walk from Charing Cross underground station and from all the buses that pass through Trafalgar Square.

Buckingham Palace is near St James's Park, Victoria or Green Park underground stations. No buses pass Buckingham Palace, but it is only a short walk from Hyde Park Corner.

7. The Royal Mews

What looks like the entrance to the Royal Mews behind Buckingham Palace — a gateway topped on each side with a lion and a unicorn — is really the exit.

The entrance is an ordinary doorway a few yards further down Buckingham Palace Road on the left. Turnstiles let you into a big quadrangle where the lamps are topped with golden crowns. Carriages, coaches, harness and the horses themselves occupy buildings on all four sides of the square.

Chief attraction is the **Gold State Coach,** used for every coronation since that of George IV. When it was made in 1762 for George III, it was described as 'very superb'. It is still very superb and is gilded all over.

The lavishly decorated framework of the coach consists of eight palm trees which branch out at the top to support the roof. There are all kinds of symbolic decorations, including, at the very top, three cherubs supporting the Royal Crown and holding the Sceptre, the Sword of State and the Ensign of Knighthood. It is drawn by eight postillion horses, and can proceed only at walking speed.

In the **State Carriage House** on the right at the end of the square are many other handsome coaches, including the Glass State Coach used for all royal weddings since the time of George V's coronation. It generally carries the bride and bridegroom from the church, as it did when the Queen (then Princess Elizabeth) married the Duke of Edinburgh.

Another coach here is Queen Alexandra's State Coach. She and Edward VII used it to attend operas, balls and banquets. It is often seen in London still, as it carries new ambassadors to Buckingham Palace to present their credentials to the Queen. It has also been used, with a cushion on a specially installed table, to carry the Imperial State Crown to the House of Lords for the opening of Parliament.

As you leave the State Carriage House, the sweet smell of hay directs you to the adjoining **stables.** On one side stand the greys — the Windsor Greys, their tails bound in pale blue; on the other are the bays — predominantly Cleveland Bays with their tails bound in red. The Windsor Greys are not a special breed. Until George V began using them in London, they were employed mainly to draw private carriages at Windsor, and thus became known as the Windsor Greys.

On the right as you go towards the exit are the **State Harness Room** and a display of saddlery. There are many historic items in these exhibits, including George IV's ornate saddle equipped with pouches for powder flasks, Queen Victoria's side saddle, and a beautiful set of hand-made pony harness presented to George V's children by the harness makers of England, and used again by Prince Charles and his brothers.

There was a king's 'mewse' in the reign of Richard II. But in those days these were places where falcons were kept during their mewing or change of plumage. That royal 'mewse' was where Trafalgar Square is today.

Admission

The Royal Mews are open every Wednesday and Thursday, 2 p.m. to 4 p.m. except when there is a carriage procession that day, at Royal Ascot or for a State Visit, for example. Admission charge. For more information telephone 01-930 4832 extension 634.

How to get there

Take the Underground to Victoria Station, which is only six minutes' walk away; or catch any bus going to Victoria.

The streets of Westminster are thickly 'peopled' with stone and bronze statues. You will recognise Sir Winston Churchill, facing the Houses of Parliament, and 'Monty', Viscount Montgomery of Alamein, on Raleigh's Lawn in Whitehall, but who was Havelock in Trafalgar Square, and had you noticed that George IV, also in the square, is riding without stirrups? 'Discovering London's Statues and Monuments' in this series describes most of them and explains why they were erected.

8. The Tower of London

Though the Tower of London has a sinister reputation, it was once London's greatest diversion. It contained the royal menagerie, begun in 1235 when Henry III installed three leopards. In 1251 came a polar bear which was allowed (at the end of a long cord) to fish in the Thames.

Today, the Tower is mainly a museum. It was once a fortress, and an almost self-contained settlement, for behind the two protective walls were a palace, the mint, the arsenal, the Crown Jewels, and a state prison. It is still maintained as an arsenal with a garrison, and during both World Wars it was used as a prison for spies, traitors and state prisoners, including Rudolf Hess (Hitler's deputy) in 1941. The palace was completely destroyed in Charles II's reign. The mint has been established elsewhere, but the Crown Jewels are still guarded and displayed at the Tower.

The Tower is a collection of Norman and medieval buildings dominated by the White Tower, built by William the Conqueror to protect (and to overawe) the citizens of London. Some of the stone was imported from Normandy.

Most of our sovereigns up to James I used the Tower as a palace, often staying there the night before their coronation. The Tower was used as a state prison as early as 1100, but it was not until Tudor and Stuart times that the threat of being sent to the Tower hung over every political figure.

The Bell Tower

The outer wall of the Tower is surrounded by a deep moat. Entrance is through the Middle Tower and the Byward Tower, passing the **Bell Tower** on the left. Here **John Fisher, Bishop of Rochester,** and **Sir Thomas More,** who both refused to acknowledge Henry VIII as supreme head of the church, were confined. Poor Fisher, in his cold imprisonment, cried out for food, clothes and warmth. But he approached the execution block with dignity — and with the New Testament in his hand. Sir Thomas met his death with a quiet jest. He moved his beard carefully from the block, 'for,' he said, 'though you have a warrant to cut off my head, you have none to cut my beard.' The **Duke of Monmouth,** the illegitimate son of Charles II, who tried to capture the throne from James II, was also imprisoned in the Bell Tower.

25

Traitors' Gate

On the right is the Traitors' Gate through which many illustrious prisoners were taken to the Tower. One such prisoner was **Princess Elizabeth,** who was rigidly confined to the Tower for two months by her sister, Queen Mary, who feared Elizabeth's influence with the Protestants. As Elizabeth stepped ashore on to the steps of Traitors' Gate, she sank down and wept — the only time in her life that she showed fear.

The Bloody Tower

Turning left, we pass under the portcullis of the Bloody Tower, the only remaining original entrance to the wall defending the Inner Ward. The archway was built by Henry III. The portcullis is still in working order.

Here, according to legend, the 'little princes', **Edward V** and **Richard of York,** were murdered in 1483. The bodies were secretly buried. Their burial place was not discovered till nearly two hundred years later, during Charles II's reign. A stairway was being demolished next to the White Tower, and the boys' bones were discovered. Charles had them reburied in Westminster Abbey.

Sir Walter Raleigh was also imprisoned in the Bloody Tower, by James I. This great seaman and explorer was confined to its close quarters for thirteen years. 'Only my father could keep such a bird in a cage!' cried young Henry, Prince of Wales. The prisoner's only exercise was pacing 'Ralegh's Walk', a few yards of wall that is still there. (He spelt his name 'Ralegh' and this spelling is used at the Tower.) He never lost the affection of Londoners, nor of the sailors who passed up and down the Thames, and Raleigh would answer their greetings from his 'walk'. The main rooms have been restored and furnished as they would have been during his imprisonment.

Another popular prisoner here was **John Felton,** the young Army lieutenant who murdered the Duke of Buckingham (the favourite of Charles I) in Portsmouth in 1628. The Duke was so unpopular that Felton had an almost triumphant entry to the Tower, and the townsfolk shouted encouragement to him all the way to his execution at Tyburn.

The Duke of Monmouth was possibly lodged in the Bloody Tower after the battle of Sedgemoor before being taken to the Bell Tower on the eve of his execution. The unscrupulous **Judge Jeffreys,** who treated Monmouth's men with such ferocity at the Bloody Assizes, was also imprisoned in this tower. (At the Assizes he sentenced over two hundred people to be hanged, and sent eight hundred into slavery in the Barbadoes.) When James II escaped to France after the landing of William of Orange, Jeffreys, disguised as a sailor, also tried to escape. But he was recognised in a tavern near Wapping by a man he had ill-treated. He was not executed but died of disease and drink.

Tower Green

Leaving the Bloody Tower and walking towards the White Tower, we come to Tower Green, where the famous ravens stalk about. The Green is in two parts. On the northern side is the site of the block, where a number of famous people were allowed the privilege of being executed in comparative privacy.

Among these were **Anne Boleyn,** the dark-haired second wife of Henry VIII (in 1536); the aged **Margaret, Countess of Salisbury** (1541); **Catherine Howard,** the fifth wife of Henry VIII, his 'rose without a thorn' (in 1542); **Lady Jane Grey,** uncrowned Queen of England for nine unhappy days (in 1554); and **Robert Devereux, Earl of Essex,** Queen Elizabeth's young favourite (in 1601).

The Countess of Salisbury had once been Queen Mary's governess. She was executed because of Tudor jealousy towards her family and her, the last of the Plantagenets. It is said the poor old countess cried out that she was no traitor, and with her long white hair streaming behind her, she ran round and round the execution block till the headsman finally caught her.

All the Tower Green victims were executed with an axe except Anne Boleyn, who persuaded Henry to allow her to be executed with a sword. Anne went to the block with great courage. She jested that history would have no difficulty in finding a nickname for her. 'They will call me', she declared, 'la royne Anne sans tete!' But she grew so bright-eyed with terror that the executioner lost his nerve. He signalled his assistant to distract Anne's attention, snatched up his sword, and beheaded her unawares.

Beauchamp Tower

Between the two sections of Tower Green is a path leading to the Beauchamp Tower (dating from Edward I), the main prison for people of rank. This tower is famous for the inscriptions carved or scratched on the walls. One of the best is a carving by **John Dudley, Earl of Warwick,** of his family badge of a lion, a bear and ragged staff (1553). He added his name *John Dvdle* and surrounded the design with a garland of roses, oak leaves, gillyflowers and honeysuckle, to represent the names of his four brothers imprisoned with him. The rose was for Ambrose, the oak for Robert (later Queen Elizabeth's favourite, the Earl of Leicester) — from *robur,* an oak, gillyflowers stood for Guildford (husband of Lady Jane Grey), and the honeysuckle for Henry.

Twice scratched on the walls is also the word *Iane,* supposed to refer to Lady Jane Grey, probably carved by Guildford Dudley or one of his brothers. Guildford was executed on Tower Hill.

From her window in the Yeoman Gaoler's quarters Lady Jane saw her husband led out to his execution, and a little later saw his body brought back to be buried in the Chapel of St Peter ad Vincula (St Peter in chains) where she too was buried after her execution later that same day. In this chapel (standing to the north of the execution site) lie Sir Thomas More, Anne Boleyn, Catharine Howard, Essex, Monmouth and many others.

The White Tower

In the centre of the eighteen acres of the Tower and its grounds stands the White Tower, its massive walls measuring from 11 to 15 feet (3.4 to 4.5 m) thick. This square-looking tower is not, in fact, square. Three of its corners are not right angles, and of the four turrets three are square and one (on the north-east) is round. The Armouries, the national museum of arms and armour, are housed here, with exhibitions on every floor. This tower also contains St John's Chapel, one of the oldest churches in London. The altar hangings were made from decorations used at Westminster Abbey for the coronation of George VI in 1937.

Arms and armour

There has always been armour in the Tower and the present collection is comprehensive and important. Particularly fine is the armour of Henry VIII, which, during his reign, was distributed between Greenwich (where there was a royal armoury), Westminster, Hampton Court and Windsor. **Henry VIII** enjoyed taking part in tournaments, and in the Armoury are several of his armours for foot combat (fought with swords or poleaxes) and for the joust (between horsemen armed with lances). Tournament armour was stronger and heavier than battle armour because mobility was less important in these formalised combats.

As a young man, Henry was slim and athletic. Only a slim man could have worn the tonlet (skirted) armour which (we now know) was made for him to wear in the tournaments at the Field of the Cloth of Gold in 1520, when Henry and his nobles met Francis I and the French nobility. Later in life Henry grew extremely fat and a very strong horse would have been needed to carry him in the suit of armour made for him at Greenwich in 1540.

Also from the royal armoury at Greenwich is the suit of armour made for Elizabeth's life-long friend and favourite, and her first Master of Horse, **Robert Dudley,** her 'Sweet Robin'. (They were imprisoned in the Tower at the same time. They had partly grown up together, and possibly they met and fell in love for the first time, during their imprisonment.)

In another case are suits of armour belonging to **Charles I** in about 1630, and to **Charles II** when he was the twelve-year-old Prince of Wales, and facing these is a cabinet containing buff coats worn by Cromwellian soldiers. By tradition, one coat belonged to **Colonel Francis Hacker,** who supervised the execution of Charles I in Whitehall on 30th January 1649.

By the time of the Restoration of Charles II, armour had become out-dated, and it was during his reign that the collection of arms and armour was begun at both the Tower and at Windsor Castle. Over the years additions have been made, and continue to be made, but the old royal nucleus is still the main focal point, giving the Armoury a special link with the history of England.

Down in the basement (at one time used as the torture chamber) are the Mortar Room, showing bronze mortars, muskets and rifles and the Cannon Room, with cannon, armour and pikes preserved in the Tower since the Civil War.

Escapes

There have always been armed men in the Tower, and prisoners were closely guarded. But there was naturally a certain amount of coming and going. Some of the prisoners were allowed visitors. (Raleigh's wife, for instance, took a house on Tower Hill, and visited him regularly during his long imprisonment, and his son Carew was born during this period). Also, tradesmen had to supply the Tower with food and fuel, and it was these permitted visits that inspired the escape of **Lord William Seymour** and Lord Nithsdale.

Seymour, who was imprisoned for marrying Arabella Stuart, a cousin of James I, bribed a carrier delivering faggots and hay to give him a smock and a large hat, and allow him to take his place on the outward journey. He walked out of the Tower and escaped to France. In 1649, bearing no grudge against the son of the king who had imprisoned him, Seymour offered to take the place of Charles I on the scaffold.

Even more daring was the escape of **Lord Nithsdale,** one of three Scottish noblemen sent to the Tower after the failure of the Jacobite Rising of 1715. On the evening before the execution, his wife and women friends smuggled a hooded cape and skirt in to her husband's room. The visitors confused the guards by going back and forth, and in the confusion Lord Nithsdale, 'weeping' convincingly, was led out by one of his wife's companions. To give him time to make his way out through the gateway of the Bloody Tower and along the walk past the Bell Tower to the main entrance, Lady Nithsdale kept up the pretence of talking to her husband — and as she was leaving, turned back a servant who was carrying candles, with the plea that Lord Nithsdale was at his devotions and wished to be alone. Lord Nithsdale escaped to Italy disguised as a servant in the Venetian Ambassador's retinue. Lady Nithsdale joined him, and together they lived happily in Rome until Lord Nithsdale died — twenty-eight years after he had been sentenced to death in the Tower.

Yeoman Warders

Always on duty at the Tower are Yeoman Warders, who act as guides when available. The Yeoman Warders number thirty-seven men from time-expired warrant and non-commissioned officers of the Army and the RAF. They are 'extraordinary members of the Queen's Bodyguard of the Yeomen of the Guard', but they form a quite separate body from the Yeoman of the Guard, which is probably the oldest permanently established royal bodyguard in the world. These royal guards were newly appointed on the accession of a new sovereign, and were known by various titles, including 'Cross Bowmen of the Household'.

Henry VII created the Yeomen of the Guard as a permanent body in 1485. During its long history, the scarlet Tudor dress and equipment has changed little, but its duties have become ceremonial and decorative. At one time the Yeomen guarded the king at home and abroad, even on the field of battle. Now their duties are confined to searching the vaults of Westminster Palace (with halberds and lamps in hand) on the day Parliament assembles (in case of another Guy Fawkes plot), and attending the sovereign at the opening of Parliament and on the day of the distribution of Maundy Money.

When Henry VIII was living in the Tower (as he did for some years) the Yeomen were in constant attendance on him. When he was away from the Tower, the fact that it was a royal residence was indicated by the twelve Yeomen who were permanently stationed there. They were the Tower Warders — and the distinction still holds good. Yeoman Warders take no part in the Court duties of the Yeomen of the Guard, whose scarlet costume is trimmed with black and gold and worn with a white ruff: their stockings are red, and their shoes are trimmed with red and white rosettes. They wear a cross-over belt (the chief difference between their costume and that of the Yeoman Warders of the Tower). On State occasions both Yeomen of the Guard and Yeomen Warders wear a Tudor garlanded hat.

The ravens

Ravens were once common in London streets, and were protected as useful scavengers. There have probably always been ravens at the Tower. They were said to fly in from the Essex marshes whenever there was an execution — and some of them stayed on. There is a legend that the Tower will collapse if the ravens leave, so some are always kept 'on the establishment'. They are cared for by a Yeoman Warden and are given a weekly allowance of horseflesh.

Crown Jewels

Many people go to the Tower solely to see the Crown Jewels, and walk straight through the Bloody Tower entrance to the Jewel House and down the four flights of stairs to see these magnificent royal treasures.

But there is much splendour to see before going down.

On the ground floor is a display of many of Britain's most famous awards, including the Victoria Cross, George Cross, Distinguished Service Order, Distinguished Service Cross, Military Cross, the Distinguished Flying Cross and the decorations and robes of various orders, like the Order of the Bath and the Order of the British Empire. Nearby are two golden coronation robes worn by every sovereign for the past 150 years, except Queen Victoria.

Also on the ground floor are a set of sixteen silver state trumpets and the Great Sword of State with its magnificent scabbard. This is carried before a sovereign as he enters Westminster Abbey for coronation, and at the State Opening of Parliament.

Most of the treasures of the Jewel House are connected with the coronation ceremony. After the execution of Charles I many of the royal ornaments were destroyed by order of Cromwell's Parliament, even the Saxon crown of Edward the Confessor — St Edward's Crown — which had been used to crown English kings for almost 400 years. Only three pieces escaped destruction: the Anointing Spoon, the Ampulla (a golden eagle holding the holy oil) and Queen Elizabeth's Salt (all three pieces are now displayed among the Crown Jewels).

A new set of crown jewels had to be made for the coronation of Charles II, and additional pieces have been added from time to time, usually following earlier designs.

Among the many crowns on show is a small diamond crown made for Queen Victoria, not much bigger than an apple, but one of the most important crowns is **St Edward's Crown** — so called after Edward the Confessor. It was made for Charles II, probably from the old crown of St Edward broken up during the

Commonwealth, but owing to its great weight (nearly 5 pounds, 2.3 kg) it is only used for the actual ceremony of coronation. It is then exchanged for the lighter **Crown of State,** which was made for the coronation of Queen Victoria and used at every coronation since then. This is also the crown worn by the sovereign for the opening of Parliament. Its oak-leaf patterned frame is set with more than three thousand precious stones, mostly diamonds and pearls. Outstanding among these jewels is the **Black Prince's ruby,** a great irregular, uncut balas-ruby as big as a pullet's egg. This magnificent ruby was worn by Henry V at the battle of Agincourt in 1415. Also in this crown is the Stuart sapphire, taken to France by James II when he fled the country, and repurchased on the death of Cardinal Henry Benedict Stuart, the last of the house. In the upper cross is a sapphire which, according to tradition, was worn by Edward the Confessor and recovered from his grave in the twelfth century.

Another beautiful crown is that made for the coronation of Queen Elizabeth the Queen Mother in 1937. It embodies the famous Indian diamond, the **Koh-i-noor** (or Mountain of Light).

It will help you to understand much of what you see if you visit the History Gallery, next to the Lanthorn Tower, where the story of the Tower from its beginning is explained in words and pictures.

Admission

From March to October, 9.30 a.m. to 5 p.m.; rest of the year 9.30 a.m. to 4 p.m.; Sundays (from March till late October), 2 p.m. to 5 p.m. (Not open on Sundays in winter).

The admission charge varies according to season. Special programmes can be organised for school visits, in some cases with free admission, and there are holiday activities. Enquiries to Education Centre, Waterloo Block, HM Tower of London, EC3N 4AB. Tel: 01-709 0765, extension 247.

How to get there

Much the easiest way is by District or Circle Line underground to Tower Hill station.

ALL HALLOWS BY-THE-TOWER

On the right, at the top of Tower Hill, is All Hallows by-the-Tower, the City's oldest church in that its foundation dates back to the time of the Saxon kings. Most of the church was destroyed in the Second World War, but the brick tower — the only example of Cromwellian architecture in London — survived and was incorporated (with a beautiful, added spire) into the rebuilt church, rededicated in 1957.

All Hallows (meaning 'All Saints') is the guild church of the Toc H movement, founded during the First World War by Dr

P. B. ('Tubby') Clayton to carry the spirit of service into the years of peace. The Toc H lamp burns in the church.

Toc H members from all over the world contributed to the rebuilding of All Hallows. New Zealand gave rimu panelling, the United States gave steel, Montreal gave a peal of eighteen bells, Canada as a whole presented tiles for the Nave. Maryborough, Queensland, where Dr Clayton was born, donated a ceremonial chair. On the back are inscribed the words: *Fashioned with Zeal for your Reverend Rest. If you find me Strong and Thorough I was made in Maryborough.*

It was from the Cromwellian tower of All Hallows that Samuel Pepys and his wife watched the Great Fire of London sweep up the street in September, 1666. The fire reached the porch of All Hallows, and was only prevented from spreading further by the action of Admiral Sir William Penn, who ordered sailors to blow up houses in the fire's path.

This William Penn was the father of the **William Penn** (1644-1718) who founded Pennsylvania. He was born on Tower Hill and christened in All Hallows. On New Year's Day in 1662, Pepys invited William Penn and his sister to visit his home in Seething Lane (near the church), where they consumed a barrel of oysters.

The London Brass Rubbing Centre has a collection of replica brasses from all parts of the country assembled here for rubbing.

9. Tower Bridge

Tower Bridge first opened on 2nd July 1894 and met with such varied opinions as 'picturesque and stately' and 'what strikes one most at present is that the whole structure is the most monstrous architectural sham that we have ever known of'. It has nevertheless become one of London's most cherished landmarks and its towers and old engine rooms are now open to the public. Each tower holds a different exhibition on the bridge's conception and history, from the various designs before it was built to proposals to reconstruct it as recent as 1943. In the North Tower, a video film shows the bridge being raised, architect's sketches are on show, a model has been constructed in cross-section, and there are some interesting statistics. Did you know that the bridge holds 11,300 tons of wrought iron and steel, slightly more than in HMS *Belfast,* or that it contains brickwork enough to build three hundred and fifty detached houses?

For children, however, the best part of the visit will be crossing the covered walkways between the upper floors of the two towers. On a clear day you can see nearly all the other landmarks of London, from the nearby Tower and Monument to the distant Victoria Tower of the Houses of Parliament and even the chimneys of Battersea Power Station.

Afterwards you can go to the Tower Bridge Museum under the bridge on the south bank. The massive boilers, steam pumps and accumulators used in raising the bridge before the conversion to electric power are now open to view.

Admission
Open 10 a.m. to 6.30 p.m. (April to October), 10 a.m. to 4.45 p.m. (November to March). Admission charge. For more information, telephone 01-407 0922.

How to get there.
Tower Hill Underground station is nearby and from there follow the signs to the bridge.

10. The Lord Mayor's Procession

One of London's finest (and entirely free) days of celebration and pageantry is the second Saturday in November—the day of the Lord Mayor's Show.

It is the day when the newly elected Lord Mayor shows himself to the people of London on his way to the Law Courts, where he is formally presented to the judges of the Queen's Bench Division.

The procession goes from the Mansion House, past St Paul's, along Fleet Street to the Law Courts, and then back again to the City along the Embankment. The floats taking part usually reflect the business interests of the new Lord Mayor, but the chief interest is the magnificent coach, built in 1757 and drawn by six perfectly matched brewers' horses. The coachman (who is so splendidly dressed in gold-laced scarlet livery that children sometimes think *he* is the Lord Mayor) wears a tricorn hat, and handles the six horses with reins of scarlet webbing. The coach itself, over 10 feet (3m) high, is resplendent with gold, crystal and scarlet. The only brake on it is a wheel-brake operated by a footman walking behind.

The coach is escorted by pikemen of the Honourable Artillery Company of Pikemen and Musketeers. This military body was granted a charter by Henry VIII, and is thus the oldest regiment in the British Army, and probably in the world. From 1537 to the present day it has provided citizen soldiers for the defence of the country. HAC men were amongst the troops inspected by Elizabeth at Tilbury in 1588. Milton, Wren and Samuel Pepys all served in this famous Company.

The HAC pikemen in the procession are dressed in 1640 uniforms and their drill is based on a drill book of 1635. To equip themselves in their Cromwellian uniform takes half an hour. They have to don stockings, knee breeches, tunic, breast plate, back plate, and a pot helmet with a swirling feather. The weight of their armour and weapons is about 25 pounds (11.3 kg).

Royal visits

The Lord Mayor is an extremely important person in the City, but it is not true (as many people think) that the sovereign has to ask his permission to enter the City. The Lord Mayor does go to the City boundary (marked by the griffin in the middle of Fleet Street) when the sovereign is visiting the City, but this is to greet her. The sovereign halts just inside the City boundary, and there the Lord Mayor advances towards the royal coach, carrying the Pearl Sword of Elizabeth I, its point lowered in submission. He surrenders it with an expression of loyalty and it is returned to him with equal courtesy. The Lord Mayor then returns to his coach and precedes the sovereign through the streets of the City.

The Pearl Sword is said to have been presented to the City by Queen Elizabeth when she visited the Exchange in 1571, and bestowed on the building the title of 'Royal Exchange'.

11. The City and its street names

When you are walking about exploring London (and really it is the only way to discover some of its secrets) take a note of the street names, for they will often tell you something of its development.

This is especially true in the City, the shape and area of which has always been much the same, ever since the building of the Roman wall, parts of which are still standing. (There is a sizeable section near Tower Hill underground station.)

The Old English word *straet* originally meant a paved street, and Henry I decreed that a street must be wide enough for sixteen knights to ride abreast. Lanes were narrower, and had only to be wide enough for two men to roll a barrel of wine along them.

Many of the London streets that were important centuries ago are still important, such as Cheapside, Poultry, Threadneedle Street, Cornhill and Lombard Street—all of them near the Bank of England.

In a walk lasting an hour or so you can discover quite a lot about old London. Start at **Ludgate Circus.**

Ludgate was one of the old gates leading into the City. There was no King Lud, as some legends say. The name probably comes from the Old English *Ludgaet,* meaning back door or postern gate.

Many of the first London names were occupational names—reminders of the kind of life that once went on. Up Ludgate Hill, on the left, are **Ave Maria Lane, Amen Court** (set back a little), **Paternoster Steps** and **Paternoster Square.** Rosary makers and scripture text writers once lived here.

Walk round to the left of St Paul's, past the statue of St Paul himself among the plane trees, and you come into **Cheapside,** once the most important street in London. *Chepe* meant market. Cheapside was once considerably wider than it is today, and everything went on there—street trading, processions, bonfires, victory celebrations, executions, and the quick-flaring riots of the apprentices. (They particularly resented foreigners. The cry would go up 'Prentices! Clubs!' and they would rush belligerently out of the shops.)

The first corner on the left off Cheapside is **Foster Lane,** from St Vedast, or St Vaast, a bishop of Arras who died about 540. (This is a good example of how names can change over the years.) Robert Herrick, the poet, was christened in St Vedast's church.

In Foster Lane is the Goldsmiths' Hall. The Goldsmiths' Company, incorporated in 1327, still assays and stamps gold and silver plate. Its hallmark is a leopard's head. Next on the left is Gutter Lane, then **Wood Street,** with an old plane tree preserved in the tiny churchyard-garden of St Peter, Chepe, destroyed in the Great Fire of London. St Peter's Keys, in gold, are incorporated into the railings round this small garden, to which there is no gateway. Set back a little from Cheapside and leading off Wood Street is **Milk Street,** where cows once grazed and milk was sold. (Sir Thomas More was born there in 1478). On the right is **Bread Street,** where bread was baked and sold. (John Milton was born there in 1608.)

Bow bells

Just past Bread Street is **St Mary-le-Bow.** Every true Cockney has to be born within the sound of Bow bells which, according to legend, encouraged Dick Whittington to return to London as he was leaving disconsolately. The bells chimed out to him: 'Turn again, turn again, thrice mayor of London'. (In fact, he became Mayor three times—in 1396, 1397-8, 1406-7, and Lord Mayor in 1419-20.)

The curfew was rung by Bow bells for over six hundred years, and a nine o'clock bell signalled the end of the working day for the apprentices.

The name of the church comes from the bows or arches on which it was originally built. It was badly blitzed, and has been

much restored. The first church had a small grandstand on the tower overlooking Cheapside, from which royalty could watch pageants and processions.There is a balcony on the tower Wren built. It holds the flagpole. Charles II once planned to watch a Lord Mayor's procession from there, but he was warned of an assassination plot and stayed away.

Beside the church is a statue of **Captain John Smith,** first governor of Virginia, whose life was saved (in 1608) by the thirteen-year-old Red Indian princess, Pocahontas. She later married Captain James Rolfe, and in 1616 became the first American to visit England. She died (of pneumonia) off Gravesend as she was returning to America. Mrs Woodrow Wilson, wife of one of the United States' presidents (1913-1921), claimed descent from Pocahontas's son Thomas Rolfe.

Guildhall

Just past St Mary-le-Bow, go up King Street to the left and ahead there is **Guildhall,** or the Hall of the Corporation of the City of London. The Guildhall, open from 10 a.m. to 5 p.m. (on Saturdays, to 4 p.m.) is now used for municipal meetings, the election of the Lord Mayor and Sheriffs, and for state banquets. Some of the building was destroyed in the Second World War, but much of the Great Hall (originally built about 1411 to 1435) dates from its restoration in the seventeenth century.

As you enter Guildhall, just opposite the entrance is a door leading to the Ambulatory. On the left are large memorials to Lord Nelson (died 1805) and Sir Winston Churchill (died 1965). Set into the floor, and on the wall opposite Churchill, are brass tablets giving the standard measurements of inches, feet and the imperial yard.

At the far end of the hall is the Musicians' Gallery, guarded at each end by the famous figures of the legendary giants, Gog and Magog. The ancestors of the present figures were made of wicker and were paraded in pageants, and their basket-work hands were used to present petitions. The present Gog and Magog are sombre creatures in green-brown war paint picked out in gold. They are over 9 feet (2.7 m) tall and weigh 15 hundredweight (762 kg).

On the dais opposite the Musicians' Gallery is held the Court of Hustings, at which liverymen from all the craft-guilds gather to elect the Lord Mayor.

37

Famous trials

Less happy occasions connected with Guildhall are commemorated on a tablet. Anne Askew, a protestant martyr, was tried there in 1540. She was tortured at the Tower, carried in a chair to Smithfield, and there burnt to death.

The most important trial was that of the fifteen-year-old Lady Jane Grey, uncrowned queen of England for nine days, and her young husband, Lord Guildford Dudley. They were executed on the same day in 1554.

The twelve great companies

The banners hanging in Guildhall belong to the twelve great livery companies—the Mercers, Grocers, Drapers, Fishmongers, Goldsmiths, Skinners, Merchant Taylors, Haberdashers, Salters, Ironmongers, Vintners and Clothworkers. (There are over seventy other companies—each formed as a kind of friendly society to look after its members, and to fix wages and standards of workmanship.)

A Tudor adventurer

In front of Guildhall runs **Gresham Street,** called after Sir Thomas Gresham, founder of the first Royal Exchange in the reign of Elizabeth I.

Thomas Gresham was the son of a Lord Mayor of London, and was a leading member of the Merchant Adventurers. He came from a leading Norfolk family, and was an able and adventurous man, with an advanced understanding of economics, which in those days was known as 'political arithmetic'. He was sent to the Low Countries and Germany to negotiate loans for the Crown with wealthy merchants, and brought back 'gonne-powder and salt-peter', handled bullion, became a kind of secret agent for Elizabeth's Lord Burghley—and for Elizabeth's half-brother, Edward VI, he brought a 'great present of a payre of long Spanish silke stockings'.

At the height of his involvement with the Crown, Gresham crossed the Channel no fewer than forty times in two years—no small adventure in itself in those days.

Proceed along Gresham Street to the left when you leave Guildhall. On the right you pass **Old Jewry.** Until the expulsion of the Jews by Edward I in 1290, this was the main Jewish quarter in London—and the word itself incorporates an old form of plural, *ry,* also used in poultry and rookery.

'The Old Lady of Threadneedle Street'

Pass the end of Old Jewry, and turn right into **Princes Street.** In the distance you can see the top of the Monument to the Great Fire of London. All along the left-hand side of Princes

Street runs part of the **Bank of England,** which stands on an island site of more than three acres. On the outside, it is completely without windows—for security's sake—and only the entrance is open to the public.

'The Old Lady of Threadneedle Street' is the Bank's affectionate nickname, but look at the pediment. There sits 'the Old Lady' herself, her mantle billowing out in the wind. There is some doubt about the origin of the word 'threadneedle'. Perhaps three needles once appeared on a hanging sign of needle makers. Another theory is that threadneedle was a children's game, like oranges and lemons.

Seven great streets meet in the triangle dominated by the Bank of England; first Princes Street, then (clockwise), Threadneedle Street, **Cornhill** (where corn was once grown), **Lombard Street, King William Street, Queen Victoria Street,** and **Poultry.** (This is a continuation of Cheapside, and marks the area where poultry sellers once set up their stalls.)

Between Threadneedle Street and Cornhill is the **Royal Exchange.** This is a replacement of the one built by Sir Thomas Gresham, but on top is still his family crest—the famous golden grasshopper.

If you go 100 yards or so down Threadneedle Street and look up at the side of the Royal Exchange, you will see two figures (unnamed). On the right, in the long robes, is Dick Whittington. The other is Hugh Myddelton, who channelled drinking water to London from Hertfordshire—a great engineering feat—in the reign of James I.

Street of signs

Cornhill is a typical big commercial city street, but it is worth walking down **Lombard Street** to see the kind of hanging signs which were, before people could read, such a decorative and useful advertising feature of London life: the Black Horse of Lloyds Bank, the Golden Grasshopper of Martins Bank, a golden anchor and rope, a golden artichoke on a green ground, the charming Cat and Fiddle of the Royal Bank of Scotland, the Black Eagle of Barclays Bank, and the three gold crowns of Coutts and Co. They all hang from wrought iron supports.

Lombard Street takes its name from the Lombards, who came to England from Lange Borde in the Lower Elbe district. When the Jews were expelled from England, the Lombards took over much of their trading and money-lending—and from the piles of unredeemed pledges which cluttered their storerooms comes the word 'lumber'.

The Mansion House and the Lord Mayor

Traffic near the Mansion House seems to come from all

directions, so cross King William Street carefully, and there is the Mansion House, with its Corinthian portico and six pillars. The Mansion House is the Lord Mayor's official residence. It has ceremonial apartments, its own court of justice, and a prison. The public is not normally allowed into the Mansion House, though special public functions are sometimes organised.

The City is really a self-contained 'kingdom' with the Lord Mayor as its ruler. It has its own police force (recognisable by their red and white striped brassards), and inside the City limits the Lord Mayor takes precedence over everyone except the sovereign. The Lord Mayor has some interesting privileges. He is the first person to be told of the sovereign's death; he is the first person to be summoned to the Privy Council when a royal succession is proclaimed; he is hereditary Butler at the coronation; he is always told the day's password to the Tower of London; he is Admiral of the Port of London—and receives a warrant for a quarter of a buck in July and a quarter of a doe in November from the royal parks.

King John was the first king to grant London the honour of electing a mayor, but he wanted to inspect the City's choice, so he declared that each mayor should pay his respects to him at Westminster Palace. That was the origin of the present Lord Mayor's procession.

The Temple of Mithras

Now walk a short way down **Queen Victoria Street,** and look at the remains of the Temple of Mithras, discovered during excavations in 1954. It was once underground and measured about 60 by 20 feet (18.3 by 6.1 m).

The temple was built in Roman London, probably by the Roman garrison about the second or third century. The Mithraic religion was mainly a soldiers' religion. It demanded courage, faithfulness and endurance, but merchants also worshipped this god who seized and killed a sacred and terrible bull—the first living creature on the earth. The dying bull's blood nourished the earth, and living things began to flourish. A carved stone altar-piece from this temple, showing Mithras slaying the bull, is now in the London Museum.

Next is **Budge Row,** an underpass for pedestrians. Budge furriers once supplied lamb skin 'fur' or coney fur, used by wealthy citizens to decorate their clothes.

The catch about Cannon Street

Turn left at **Queen Street** (probably called after Charles II's queen, Catharine of Braganza), and you come to **Cannon Street.** This is one of the street names with a catch in it! It has nothing to do with cannon or cannonballs. It was originally one of the 'occupational' streets and took its name from the wax chandlers and candlewick makers who worked there. Its Old English derivation was *candelwyrtha,* meaning a candlewright. John Stow, the Elizabethan chronicler, knew it as Candelweeke Street. By the time Samuel Pepys was writing in his diary some sixty years or so later, it had already become Canning Street—and from Canning to Cannon was an easy transition.

Turn back a short way up Cannon Street to look at the famous and somewhat mysterious **London Stone** set in the side of a building opposite the entrance to Cannon Street station. It is believed to have been used by the Romans as a central stone from which to measure road distances.

Next, turn on your tracks, past the Mansion House underground station, and you are back again in Queen Victoria Street. Keep left and after crossing Bread Street, turn right into **Friday Street,** now quite a short street but once the busy and smelly centre of the fish trade. (Fridays were celebrated as meatless days in memory of Good Friday.)

City of London Information Centre

Up Friday Street, and there is Cannon Street again. Turn left, and a short distance away is the circular Information Centre opposite St Paul's. This centre is open on Mondays to Fridays from 9.30 a.m. to 5 p.m., and on Saturdays from 10 a.m. to 12.30 p.m. (01-606 3030). From here you can return to St Paul's and to Ludgate Circus, where you began.

12. The Monument

Although the Monument is almost encircled by buildings, it is so tall it can be seen from many different City streets, and anyone with enough energy to climb 311 steps will be rewarded with a fine and wide view of the City and the river. At its top is an enclosed platform, and above that is a flaming gilt urn.

The Monument was built by Sir Christopher Wren to commemorate the Great Fire of London in 1666. It is a hollow fluted Doric column of Portland stone, 202 feet (61.6 m) in height — which is said to be the distance from its base to the site of the baker's shop in Pudding Lane where the Great Fire broke out.

Admission

The Monument is in Fish Street Hill, near the northern end of London Bridge. Admission charge. From April to September it is open Mondays to Fridays from 9 a.m. to 5.40 p.m., Saturdays and Sundays from 2 p.m. to 5.40 p.m. From October to March it opens Mondays to Saturdays from 9 a.m. to 1.30 p.m., 2 p.m. to 3.40 p.m. and is closed on Sundays.

How to get there

The easiest way is to take the underground to the Monument station—the Monument itself is only a few minutes' walk away down the hill.

13. St Paul's Cathedral

When Sir Christopher Wren demolished the burnt-out ruins of Old St Paul's after the Great Fire of London with gunpowder and a battering ram, he found four layers of history on the cleared site.

The first church, founded in the early seventh century, was destroyed by fire. The second church, built of stone, was destroyed by the Vikings in the ninth century. The next church was burnt down in 1087. This was replaced by the Norman church, begun in the reign of William Rufus, which since the building of Wren's cathedral, has always been referred to as Old St Paul's.

Old St Paul's

Old St Paul's, even larger than the present one, took nearly two hundred years to build. During the fifteenth century trials for heresy and witchcraft were held in it, and those found guilty were burnt at the stake in Smithfield. But the building also witnessed ceremonies of great splendour, including the marriage of Arthur, Prince of Wales (Henry VIII's elder brother), to Catharine of Aragon in 1501.

In Elizabeth's reign the great spire, over 480 feet (146 m) tall, was struck by lightning and never restored. But the old church saw another great ceremony before it fell into final neglect and decay. Elizabeth attended a thanksgiving service there for the English victory over the Spanish Armada. With a fanfare of trumpets, she was driven right into the cathedral in a chariot drawn by four white horses.

In spite of some reconstruction, the church became a disreputable meeting place and gaming house. The nave was called 'Paul's Walk'. Men fought duels there, sold vegetables and coal, hired cut-throats and vagabonds, and led their horses through the building.

The ruin was completed during the Civil War, when Cromwell stabled his troopers' horses in the nave, and the men burnt the carved woodwork as firewood.

Wren's double dome

After the Great Fire, Christopher Wren (appointed Surveyor General and Architect by Charles II) was asked to design a new St Paul's. His building was begun in 1675; the last stone was placed in position in 1710.

Throughout those thirty-five years Wren supervised the building of this great cathedral — and at the same time, the building of some fifty other City churches. Two or three times a week he was 'dragged up and down in a basket' to see how the work was progressing. By the time the famous dome was completed, Wren was an old man, too old to fix the last stone himself, and his son had the honour of placing it in position.

When he was eighty-six, Wren retired to his house at Hampton Court, but every year till his death in 1723, in his ninety-first year, he used to go and sit in silent contemplation of the **dome.** He is buried in the Crypt, where his epitaph, written by his son, reads: *Si monumentum requiris, circumspice.* 'If you would seek his monument, look around you'.

The dome *is* St Paul's to many people. It is, in fact, a double dome. The outer one is of wood covered with lead. The elegant stone lantern on the very top, bearing a gilt ball 6 yards (5.5 m) round and a cross 365 feet (111 m) above the ground, is not supported by the outer dome, but by an unseen brick cone rising from the inner dome. The ceiling of this inner dome, which is 218 feet (66 m) high, is decorated with scenes from the life of St Paul.

Immediately beneath the great dome is a tablet marking the spot where the catafalque of Sir Winston Churchill stood during his state funeral in 1965.

The famous **Whispering Gallery** runs round the inside of the dome. What is whispered close to the wall on one side may be heard distinctly on the other side of the gallery.

Famous craftsmen

Part of Wren's genius lay in his ability to choose first-class artists and craftsmen to work with him. Chief among these were Grinling Gibbons, the woodworker who carved the organ case and wooden choir stalls, Charles Hopson, the joiner, who supervised the construction of the oak organ cases and the choir stalls, and Jean Tijou, responsible for the magnificent wrought iron sanctuary gates.

The **west front** of St Paul's (facing Ludgate Hill) has a lower colonnade of twelve columns and an upper colonnade of eight columns. They are flanked by two bell towers. In the north-west tower is a peal of twelve bells. In the south-west tower is a clock face 17 feet (5.2 m) in diameter — and 'Great Paul', one of the largest bells in England. It is rung every day at 1 p.m. It also tolls for two hours on the death of a sovereign, and for one hour on

43

the death of the Archbishop of Canterbury, the Bishop of London, the Dean of St Paul's, and the Lord Mayor.

'I shall rise again'

On the pediment of the great south door is a carving showing a **phoenix** rising from the flames. Beneath the phoenix is the word *Resurgam*. This recalls an incident that happened when measurements for the building were being made on the cleared site.

Wren asked a labourer to bring him a stone to mark the centre of his proposed dome. By chance the man picked up part of an old, damaged tombstone. On it was the one word *Resurgam* ('I shall rise again'). Wren was so impressed by this incident that he commemorated it on his new church.

To appreciate the full beauty and glory of St Paul's, stand first at the west end, just inside the main door, and look right down the nave to the marble High Altar and through the baldachino to the stained glass windows of the American War Memorial Chapel.

Then walk along the nave, past the huge Wellington memorial, to the great space beneath the dome.

Here you see the wonderful dome soaring above you, the spandrels decorated in mosaics, the lower arches showing the Crucifixion, the Entombment, the Resurrection and the Ascension.

A lion on guard

Much of the clutter of old memorials has been removed from the cathedral. The few still remaining are dominated by the pillared memorial to the Duke of Wellington (died 1852). This huge structure took twenty years to complete and is topped by the equestrian figure of Wellington himself.

In the South Transept (under the dome) is a memorial to Lord Nelson, showing Britannia pointing him out to two young boys, while the British lion lies on guard, snarling. Near the entrance to the Crypt is a memorial to Admiral Collingwood (died 1810), who took over from Nelson at the battle of Trafalgar.

The entrance to the **choir aisles** is on the north side, through fine iron gates by Jean Tijou. Beside the entrance stands a statue of Samuel Johnson (1784), the great lexicographer, in a Roman toga.

In this north aisle is the rear of the choir stalls, carved by Grinling Gibbons in the same meticulous way that he carved the front, and more beautiful Tijou gates, made from Sussex iron, splendid in black and gold with cherubs' heads, scrolls and acanthus leaves.

At the end of this aisle is the little **Chapel of Modern Martyrs,** which commemorates all known people who since 1850 have 'suffered death rather than renounce Christ'.

A step from this chapel leads to the **American War Memorial Chapel.** The floor has the words: *To the American Dead of the Second World War from the People of Britain.* A roll of honour in a glass and gold case records the names — hand-written on 473 pages of vellum — of 28,000 United States citizens serving with the Canadian, British and US Armed Forces, who lost their lives between 1941 and 1945.

The walls of this chapel, formed by the outward curve of the apse, are lined up to the windows in English oak. Some of the panelling is delicately carved with festoons in limewood showing American flowers, fruit and birds, including a scrub jay, a scarlet tanager, an osprey, a quail, and a bobolink. Rising from the top of the panelling is an American eagle.

Passing through the American War Memorial Chapel and behind the High Altar (itself a memorial to members of the Commonwealth who died in the two World Wars) we come to the **Lady Chapel.** Here the Virgin and Child are framed in part of Wren's original organ screen.

A relic of the fire

In the south choir aisle is the memorial to John Donne, Dean of St Paul's in Charles I's reign. It was scorched in the fire that burnt down Old St Paul's. And inserted into the walls nearby is a fragment of the Temple of Herod.

In the south nave aisle is Holman Hunt's picture of Christ called *The Light of the World,* and at the west end of the nave is the **Chapel of St Michael and St George,** hung with banners of the Knights of the Grand Cross (GCMG).

Opposite this, in the north aisle, are **All Souls' Chapel** and the oval **Chapel of St Dunstan.** The All Souls' Chapel contains the Kitchener Memorial, with a recumbent white marble figure of the Field Marshal (lost at sea in 1916 when the cruiser *Hampshire* struck a German mine off the Orkney Islands when Kitchener was on his way to Russia). The two silver candlesticks at the side of this altar were made from trophies won by members of the Royal Rifle Brigade who were killed in the First World War.

The Crypt

The Crypt of St Paul's has a quiet dignity, enhanced by the simplicity of the tombs and memorials.

Immediately below the dome is the tomb of Lord Nelson. He

lies in a coffin made from the mainmast of the French ship *L'Orient,* enclosed in a sarcophagus of black and white marble. It was originally part of a tomb designed for Cardinal Wolsey, the original owner of Hampton Court. When Wolsey fell from favour, Henry VIII confiscated the tomb — and forgot about it. It was found at Windsor and used for Nelson's tomb.

Also in the Crypt is Wellington's tomb, a massive sarcophagus of Cornish porphyry standing on a granite base with lions' heads sunk into each corner.

There are various bays in the Crypt devoted to sailors, soldiers, musicians and writers. Around Nelson lie famous seamen of another century, including Admiral Lord Jellicoe, Sir Roger Keyes, Earl Beatty and Sir Philip Vian.

One of the most interesting memorials in the Crypt is a link between the present St Paul's and Old St Paul's. This is a slab erected 'to Famous Dead buried in Old St Paul's or whose memorials perished'. Among the names are poor Ethelred the Unready (1016), and Sir Philip Sidney (1586), hit by a musket shot at the battle of Zutphen. Thirsty with the pain of his shattered thigh, Sidney was offered a drink of water. He turned to another dying soldier, saying: 'Thy need is greater than mine!'

The Treasury of the Diocese of London is also situated in the Crypt and contains a fascinating display of ecclesiastical chalices, patens and flagons, together with the Jubilee Cape and vestments and treasures of the cathedral. In the nave of the Crypt, Sir Christopher Wren's great model can also be seen. This marvellous wooden model was Wren's second design which, although rejected, has many recognisable features.

Admission

St Paul's is open daily, 8 a.m. to 6 p.m. Visitors may walk about at will, except on Sundays or when a service is in progress.

The Crypt is open every weekday, 10 a.m. to 4.15 p.m. (admission charge).

The Whispering Gallery, Stone Gallery and Golden Gallery are open 10 a.m. to 4.15 p.m. (admission charge). For further details telephone 01-248 2705.

14. The Museum of London

Standing high on London Wall in a corner of the Barbican raised walkway, near St Paul's, is London's own museum. Arranged on two floors surrounding a central glassed-in courtyard the displays tell the chronological story of London.

The light in the galleries is enticingly subdued, all the light being directed on to the exhibits. The story opens with the Old Stone Age people of the Upper Thames 250,000 years ago, with

Alan Sorell's pictures reconstructing convincingly how they might have looked and how they lived. Then look for the remarkable temple excavated at Heathrow and see what beautiful bronze weapons and armour were being made about the time Julius Caesar came.

Life in Roman London

When the victorious Romans built a bridge over the Thames, London was founded. The Roman section of the museum is superb. From the house interior to the cutler's stall, most items are familiar: it would not be too difficult to live as a fairly well-off city-dwelling Roman. But look for the tiny seal boxes, secured to ensure that no one looked at the message, and at the legionary's armour which it must have been such a relief to remove!

After the Romans withdrew, the Saxons had little use for London and there is little record until the decayed defences of the city were renewed as protection against the Danes (there is an impressive array of Danish battle axes and spearheads) and the city started to grow, slowly. By 1066, with its own militia, London was strong enough to force William the Conqueror to build castles to overawe his subjects, such as the White Tower, a model of which you can see here.

A jeweller's hoard

From the medieval section onwards, the displays are as varied and rich as the city itself was becoming. It would have been foolhardy to wear the lovely long pointed slippers to walk the filthy streets—look for the wooden pattens worn to raise the feet above the mud. The Cheapside hoard, buried by a jeweller, probably during an outbreak of the plague in 1603, shows exactly what he was offering for sale. **Old London Bridge** is beautifully recreated in John B. Thorp's diorama.

Before you experience the **Fire of London** at the end of this floor look out for Charles I's boots (very neat) and the tennis ball made of leather and stuffed with dog's hair. (There is a fire engine, too, after the Fire!).

Appropriately everything seems bigger downstairs in rebuilt London, as you move from the eighteenth through to the twentieth century, through rooms and offices and past shops. There are examples of every kind of fine workmanship: wealthy Londoners could afford the best. The cell door from **Newgate Prison** is a sombre reminder of those who failed. Look for the late Stuart surgical instruments. One hopes the surgeon knew more about the body than the little white figure suggests!

Our century starts with the suffragettes—the only place where you will find a Liberal cat with a woman in its mouth—quickly followed by a dark war scene with a Zeppelin in the sky. The gaiety of the thirties gives way to the 1939-45 war—look for the story of the fire bomb—and the final magnificent exhibit—the **Lord Mayor's coach.** It stands, surrounded by water to keep the wood moist, awaiting the raising of the drawbridge ahead when it is taken out for the Lord Mayor's Show in November.

The museum has a restaurant serving meals.

Admission

Open Tuesday to Saturday 10 a.m. to 6 p.m. and on Sundays 2 p.m. to 6 p.m. Closed every Monday including Bank Holiday Mondays, also Christmas Day, Boxing Day, New Year's Day. For full Christmas/New Year arrangements please telephone the Press Office. There are special facilities for school parties, which must be booked in advance through the Education Officer. Those who cannot climb the steps to the high walk should telephone for special directions. Three wheelchairs and nine pushchairs may be borrowed. Blind visitors should telephone in advance. The telephone number is 01-600 3699.

How to get there

Three underground stations, Barbican, Moorgate and St Paul's are close by, as are buses 8, 22, 25, 43 and 11.

THE BARBICAN CENTRE

Ten years in construction, the Barbican Centre was built by the City of London at a cost of £153 million and is a unique complex combining under one roof facilities for both arts and conferences. You may just like to go for a stroll and look at the unusual architecture or sit on the Lakeside Terrace and visit the Waterside Cafe, and even if you are not attending a concert, a play or a film, there are exhibitions in the Art Gallery, as well as several open exhibitions and, often, free musical entertainment in the main foyer. Visit, too, the Centre's magnificent Conservatory (open only at weekends and on public holidays), full of trees, shrubs and flowers. You can always find something to do on the Barbican's 20 acres (8 ha) of floor space. Did you know that it contains 75 miles (121 km) of pipework and enough concrete to build over 19 miles (31 km) of six lane motorways? The Centre is open from 9 a.m. throughout the week and from mid day on Sundays and Bank Holidays. A Children's Cinema Club shows special features and cartoons every Saturday. There is parking space for five hundred cars, but Moorgate and Barbican underground stations are a few minutes walk away and St Paul's, Bank and Liverpool Street underground stations are all close by. The Centre is signposted from all of these. For information telephone 01-638 4141 and for box office reservations and enquiries telephone 01-628 8795 or 01-638 8891.

15. The London Dungeon

Devised especially for those who want to know what it was really like, here is an exhibition of the gruesome and gory side of history from pagan times until the end of the seventeenth century, housed in dark chilly vaults under London Bridge station. Historically accurate, it tells a cruel yet illuminating story.

Hanged, drawn and quartered

As you enter and are faced with a bloody Halifax gibbet (not unlike a guillotine), you are immediately aware of the sombre and forbidding atmosphere. The high arches that support the railway station above tower ominously over you in candlelit darkness and exude a musty smell. Water drips to the floor, voices cry out of the blackness, a skeleton on a gibbet hangs from the stonework. The scene acclimatises you perfectly for the horrors around. Think at random of a gruesome means of death or torture and you will probably see it here, whether it is being boiled, beheaded, crucified, put on the rack, hanged, drawn and quartered, even having your hat nailed to your head. And to add to the horror, just remember that all these incidents are taken from history and have actually happened! Some of the tableaux reinforce this idea by showing the deaths of famous people, like King Harold, Richard the Lionheart and Thomas à Becket. Genuine relics of the past are also on show. Look for the frighteningly small prison door behind which captives from the Battle of Waterloo were kept.

The Plague

The most pitiful scenes are probably those of Little Ease, an oubliette in the nearby Tower of London which was too small for the occupant even to straighten his back or legs, and the plague-ravaged home of a poor family with its haunting cry of a dying baby: here the squalor and misery of disease are conveyed as clearly as the more obvious horrors of the tortures elsewhere.

Pandemonium

The one fantasy exhibit in the Dungeon is called Pandemonium. As you approach the glaring eyes of the monster painted on the door which leads to it, a sign warns that this is not for those of a nervous disposition and skulls begin to stud the walls. Inside, a tall mound rotates in front of you and as your eyes become accustomed to the deeper darkness you can pick out the monsters sprawling on top of each other which form the mound and the Devil, ready to pounce, snarling down from the top. Go through the opening in the wall in the shape of a gaping mouth into the next room. Here stands the Devil, nearly 30 feet (9m) in height. His mouth seems to move and he warns of the dire consequences awaiting those who stray from the paths of righteousness! The whole display is extremely impressive. Go past the Countess Bathery bathing in blood and return to the earthly horrors of the rest of the Dungeon.

Admission

Open daily 10 a.m. to 5.30 p.m. (April to September), 10 a.m. to 4.30 p.m. (October to March). Admission charge. Discounts for groups. The Dungeon's telephone number is 01-403 0606.

How to get there

The London Dungeon is at 28/34 Tooley Street, SE1 (appropriately the home of the notorious torturer, Roland Topcliffe). London Bridge main line and underground stations are two minutes walk away. Buses which pass nearby are 35, 44, 48, 70, 133, 501 and 513 (Monday to Friday).

16. HMS Belfast

Two hundred yards upstream from Tower Bridge and opposite the Tower of London, HMS *Belfast* has been moored since 1971. She was launched on 17th March 1938 but was soon badly damaged in the war by a German magnetic mine and had to be almost completely rebuilt. Returning to sea in 1942, she finally became flagship and took part in such celebrated battles as the sinking of the *Scharnhorst* and the D-Day landings. Outdated by 1967 she was saved from the scrapyard by the Imperial War Museum and was soon opened to the public.

Battle of North Cape

A tour of HMS *Belfast* takes you over all of the ship and shows you each aspect of its various functions. There are numerous guns arrayed on her deck, the largest of which can fire at a range of fourteen miles using shells weighing 112 pounds (50 kg) — these were loaded by hand. The **operations room** is equipped with displays on which information about friendly and enemy forces in the area were shown and these have been reconstructed in accordance with the situation at the 1943 Battle of North Cape, when the *Scharnhorst* was sunk.

Among the compartments below deck are the two **punishment cells** where offenders could be confined for up to a fortnight; the forward engine room which, with the after engine room, could propel the ship at a maximum speed of 32 knots, the two messdecks, one of 1939, the other modern. Here the sailors would spend their leisure time and it is interesting to contrast the two. In 1939 hammocks were slung across the compartment at night and there was little space. Today, separate sleeping accommodation is provided, along with recreation areas, panelling instead of bare metal, and even a choice of colour schemes.

Mine warfare

There is a mine warfare display with a dummy diver making safe a German mine, and exhibitions depicting the history of the battleship and the roles of the British cruisers in the two World Wars. A permanent exhibition is now open entitled 'Ruling the Waves' and describes the role of the Royal Family in the Royal Navy.

Admission

Open 11 a.m. to 5.50 p.m. April to October and 11 a.m. to 4.30 p.m. November to March. Closed New Year's Day, Good Friday, the first Monday in May, Christmas Eve, Christmas Day and Boxing Day. Admission charge. Telephone: 01-407 6434.

How to get there

HMS *Belfast* is moored on the Thames opposite the Tower of London. Tower Bridge and London Bridge underground stations are five minutes' walk away. There are car and coach parks nearby, or take a bus to Tower Bridge. A ferry operates from Tower Pier to HMS *Belfast*.

17. The National Theatre

Although the National Theatre was not opened until 1976, plans for its construction were begun as long ago as 1903 when William Archer and Harley Granville-Barker put forward the first detailed scheme. Work started on the building in 1969 with the aim of replacing the Old Vic as the home of the National Theatre Company which had been founded seven years before with Sir Laurence Olivier, now Lord Olivier, as director. When the complex opened, the critic Bernard Levin called it 'the finest national theatre in the world' and now guided tours give the public a chance to go behind the scenes and find out how much painstaking work goes into the production of a play.

Large enough for a double-decker bus

Each tour lasts about an hour and starts at the Lyttelton Information Desk in the foyer. From there you go up into the **Olivier Theatre.** This is the largest of the building's three auditoria and seats 1,160 people in comfortable chairs upholstered in purple (purple being Lord Olivier's favourite colour). Situated above the stage there is an enormous 'fly tower' from which large pieces of scenery can be lowered and raised, up to the weight and size of a double-decker bus, though such capacity has not been needed yet!

'Ripple' seats

From here you go down to the smaller **Lyttleton Theatre** seating 890 people. This has a movable stage which can be lifted or tilted depending on the demands of each play, and at the back of the hall are glass booths from which sound effects and lighting are controlled with the aid of computers. The first two rows of seats are sold cheaply on the day of the performance and are called 'ripple' seats. This was an idea instigated by Lord Olivier. Instead of having the first rows occupied by wealthy socialites, he preferred to have them filled with ardent theatre-goers who would have to queue for tickets early in the morning. They would react fully to the play and their response would *ripple* back through the other rows.

Behind the scenes

The tour next goes backstage at the Lyttelton Theatre, where the scenery of the plays in production can be seen. Look above the stage and you can see the various backdrops hanging from the ceiling. Then walk down the internal roadway which runs along the entire length of the back of the building and links all three theatres. Off this are rehearsal rooms, the armoury and other workshops. All of the theatre's 'props' are made on the premises, which saves money and is convenient if alterations have to be made. The painting of the backdrops, for instance, is carried out on an enormous frame with three small lifts by its side that take the painters all over the large piece of hanging material. The roof is made of glass and is slanted towards the north because the northern light is the best to paint by, and large electric fans on the walls help to dry the paint quickly.

After going through the maze of dressing rooms, you come to the building's smallest auditorium, the **Cottesloe Theatre,** which can hold up to four hundred people. It is painted in black and has the advantage of removable seats. When these are taken out the stage can be extended across the whole of the theatre and 'promenades' are given in which the public mingles with the actors, the ultimate in audience participation.

The tour ends back in the foyer, but there is always something to do in the National Theatre. There are free recitals, exhibitions, bookstalls, five buffets and, in the summer, events outside. Next door is the National Film Theatre which shows a wide range of films.

Admission

Tours begin at 10.15 a.m., 12.30 p.m., 12.45 p.m., 5.30 p.m., 6.00 p.m., except on Olivier Theatre matinee days when they begin at 10.15 a.m., 12.45 p.m. and 5.45 p.m. There are no tours on Sundays. Each tour is limited to thirty people and should be booked in advance. For further information telephone 01-633 0880. Admission charge (reductions for groups).

How to get there
Waterloo underground and main line stations are nearby and from these follow the signs to the theatre.

BRASS RUBBING
If you have ever taken a copy of the design on a coin by putting paper over it and scribbling hard with a pencil until the picture comes up you have the basic idea of brass rubbing. English churches have a variety of memorial figures of all sorts of people from knights in armour to small children: reproductions of these have been made in metal and are now collected together in brass rubbing centres so that you can choose your subject and do the rubbing without travelling to the church. There is a fee for each rubbing you take, depending upon the size of the brass, and the fee includes all the materials, the paper and wax (called Heelball) that you use. There is expert guidance and helpful advice available so that the complete beginner can achieve a very satisfactory result first go, and come away with an attractive wall decoration that is all his own work. The brass rubbing centres get very busy during the summer and it is best to arrive early to have the widest choice of brasses to rub.

At present there are collections at St James's Church, Piccadilly, 10 a.m. to 6 p.m. (12 noon to 6 p.m. Sunday), only closed on Christmas Day, at All Hallows Church beside the Tower of London, 11 a.m. to 5.45 p.m. (12.30 p.m. to 5.45 p.m. Sunday) and Westminster Abbey.

18. The Imperial War Museum
In the Imperial War Museum you will be able to find out about the two World Wars and other military operations in which Britain and the Commonwealth have been involved since 1914. Guarding the entrance to the Museum are two 15-inch (380 cm) guns, each weighing 100 tons, from the battleships *Ramillies* and *Resolution*.

A wide range of weapons and equipment is on display. There are also models, decorations, uniforms, posters, photographs and paintings. You can see a Mark V tank, a Battle of Britain Spitfire, a German one-man submarine and the rifle carried by

Lawrence of Arabia, as well as the fuselage of a Lancaster bomber and *Tamzine*, one of the 'little ships' used to rescue troops at Dunkirk.

Admission

The Imperial War Museum is open from Monday to Saturday from 10 a.m. to 5.50 p.m. and on Sunday from 2 p.m. to 5.50 p.m. The Museum is closed on New Year's Day, Good Friday, May Day bank holiday, Christmas Eve, Christmas Day and Boxing Day. Admission is free. For any other information please telephone 01-735 8922.

How to get there

The museum is in Lambeth Road, London SE1, and the nearest underground stations are Lambeth North and Elephant and Castle. Buses include nos. 3, 10, 44, 59, 109, 133, 155, 159, 172, 177 and 184.

KATHLEEN & MAY

Berthed in St Mary Overy Dock, close to Southwark Cathedral and adjacent to the river Thames on the south bank, lies the last wooden topsail schooner 'Kathleen & May', with an exhibition on board telling the story of the schooners and ketches which carried Britain's cargoes around the coasts in the nineteenth and early twentieth centuries. There is also an audio-visual display with rare film of the 'Kathleen & May' sailing. The schooner is 98 feet (30 m) in length and could carry 226 tons of cargo. The first vessel purchased by the Maritime Trust for restoration, she was initially on display in Plymouth until 1978 when she was towed to London to St Katharine's Dock. In 1985 she was moved to St Mary Overy Dock, which was specially modified to enable her to be dry-docked to allow repairs to her underwater hull. You may sometimes be able to see this work in progress but normally she will be kept afloat in the Dock.

'Kathleen & May' is open every day of the year except for Christmas Eve, Christmas Day, Boxing Day, New Year's Eve and New Year's Day, from 10 a.m. to 5 p.m. in summer and 11 a.m. to 4 p.m. in winter. Last admissions 45 minutes before closing time. Admission charge, with reductions for groups. Telephone 01-403 3965. The nearest British Rail/Underground station is London Bridge. Buses 47 and 70.

19. The National Maritime Museum and Greenwich

With Greenwich Park in the background and the Old Royal Observatory up the hill, the buildings of the National Maritime Museum are a splendid sight. Greenwich has been a centre of nautical studies since 1675 and research continues today beyond the public galleries of what is the largest museum of its kind in the world.

The West Wing is a good place to start, for the information desk and main bookshop are here. Stairs opposite the entrance doors lead to the galleries. Downstairs you find the enormous **Neptune Hall** and dominating it is the 100 foot (30 m) long steam paddle tug *Reliant*, complete with port paddle and (now electrically powered) machinery, both of which can be seen in action most afternoons. You can go aboard, stand in the engine room and see the crew's quarters through glass panels in the side. Seen from the bow of the *Reliant,* the *Donola* appears to be lying alongside the platform — she is a steam launch in perfect working order and could be steamed on the river again.

All round the hall there are magnificent figureheads and displays showing how wooden boats developed from early times down to today and there are three perfect examples of racing dinghies. Be sure to go and see the gallery under the upper platform which has detailed dioramas on cargo handling and steel shipbuilding, including Roman, medieval and eighteenth-century English ports and the building of Brunel's *Great Eastern*. Every detail is there, from Roman tally sticks to workmen's sandwiches. As a contrast, find the model container port.

A prince's floating coach

Go on to see the magnificent 'floating coach' next door — the splendid barge designed by William Kent for Frederick, Prince of Wales, in 1732. It is 63 feet (19 m) long, needed twenty-two oarsmen and was ornately carved and gilded by the greatest experts in the country.

The first gallery beyond the Barge House shows how boatbuilding changed in the fifteenth century: constructing a skeleton to be enclosed in timber enabled the builders to make boats which were larger, less rigid and more seaworthy, capable of carrying the great explorers on their voyages of discovery.

In the next gallery you will find the shadow of an ancient boat: when archaeologists investigated the Sutton Hoo burial mound they found that the wood had disappeared but were able to uncover the shape, punctuated by iron nails. How they did it and what it looked like is reconstructed in a full scale model. Other models show one of the Ferriby boats (the oldest plank boats in Europe) and the ninth-century Graveney boat.

Beyond the next gallery, which is all about yachts, there is an unusual gallery, where, beside a large model of the gunship *Cornwallis,* there are a number of audio-visual displays each devoted to an aspect of working a sailing ship.

Discovery and seapower

Return to the entrance hall and go up the main staircase to a gallery opened in October 1986 by HRH the Princess of Wales, entitled *Discovery and Seapower 1450-1700.* Here you can trace Britain's momentous transition from a small unimportant island in 1500 to its position by the end of the seventeenth century as one of the greatest naval and commercial powers in Europe. It begins with the voyages of discovery and then traces the origins of the Royal Navy under Henry VIII, and the exploits of Elizabethan seamen like Drake and Hawkins.

Among the exhibits on display are several items from the *Mary Rose,* including a magnificent bronze gun, down whose formidable 5½ inch bore visitors peer as they first enter the gallery. Other exhibits include weapons and fine pictures of the Armada and from the Stuart period come superb ship models and the great Dutch marine paintings. You can begin or end your tour by watching an audio-visual programme in the rest area adjoining the gallery.

As well as the objects on display, the gallery's design also makes the most of its position overlooking Greenwich Royal Park. A viewing platform has been built into one of the high window bays offering splendid views of the Old Royal Observatory.

A nine-year-old convict

If you descend the staircase after *Discovery and Seapower,* you will come to an exhibition based around five large liner models in the museum's collection, celebrating the 150th anniversary of the Peninsular and Oriental Steam Navigation Company. This shows how, in the pre-airliner days of the British Empire, P & O represented a vital life-line between Britain and her colonies east of Suez, and how the company has diversified in post-colonial years up to the present day.

Retrace your steps up the staircase to the middle floor level of the West Wing and you will find galleries devoted to Cook and

Nelson. The Cook Gallery illustrates the great explorer's voyages to the Pacific, and also describes the sailing of 'The First Fleet', carrying the first deportees sent from Britain to the new penal colonies of Australia. Look for the terrestrial globe as it appeared before Cook's discoveries, and see the list of convicts sent 'Down Under' two hundred years ago, the youngest a chimney sweep only nine years old!

The uniform Nelson wore at Trafalgar

The last two galleries on the middle level centre around Horatio Nelson. You can compare how he wrote with his right hand and, after he lost his arm, how well he managed with his left, how he lived aboard ship and his life at home at Merton — look for his dinner service with his coat of arms on each piece. Turner's great painting of the battle of Trafalgar shows the confusion of the great sea battle in which Nelson died. His coat, bearing the hole made by the fatal musket ball fired by a French sniper, bloodstained breeches and stockings are displayed here. Round the corner is a model of his funeral carriage and on the wall to the right its figurehead.

The path from the West Wing to the East Wing follows the old Deptford to Woolwich road and the lovely **Queen's House** was built on each side and over it. Started by Inigo Jones for Anne, wife of James I, it was finished for Henrietta Maria, wife of Charles I. The House is closed while extensive building work is being carried out and the East Wing reopens in 1988 with a major exhibition, *Armada*.

How to stand in two hemispheres at once

The **Old Royal Observatory** is one of our proudest scientific monuments and the home of Greenwich Mean Time, to which all time over the world still relates — check GMT on the twenty-four hour clock near the gate as you go in. On top of Flamsteed House — built by Christopher Wren for John Flamsteed, the first Astronomer Royal — is the red time ball which has dropped at 1 p.m. precisely since 1833 to provide a chronometer check for ships on the river. A brass strip runs across the courtyard in front of the Meridian Building, marking the Prime Meridian of the world, where the eastern and western hemispheres meet — put one foot on each side and you will be standing in two hemispheres at the same time. In the building you can see Airy's Transit Instrument (telescope and circle), which still defines the Prime Meridian. From the Dyson Gallery you can go up into the Observatory dome to see the 28 inch C telescope which is the largest refractory telescope in Britain.

The Octagon Room in Flamsteed House was built high with long narrow windows to accommodate Thomas Tompion's clocks and pendulums on the walls and maximum movement up and down for telescopes like the ones on show. Visit the **Maskelyne Gallery** to see the collection of sundials in many forms, the earliest form of timekeeping, and the Spencer Jones Gallery, where there is a display on the atomic clock.

The Greenwich Planetarium

The dome of the nearby South Building houses the Greenwich Planetarium, open to pre-booked and school parties during term and to the public on Tuesdays, Thursdays and Fridays at 2.30 and 3.30 p.m. during holidays and on Saturdays from April to August, for special programmes at stated times.

The centre for school children, called the Half Deck. is in the West Wing and can be booked in advance for school parties in term time through the Schools Liaison Officer, who will also help to arrange a suitable programme, which may include film shows, lectures or a visit to the Planetarium. Contact the Education Services Section, National Maritime Museum, Greenwich, London SE10 9NF.

Admission

The National Maritime Museum is open from 10 a.m. to 6 p.m. on weekdays (but closes at 5 p.m. from November to the Thursday before Good Friday) and from 2 p.m. to 6 p.m. on Sundays (5 p.m. in winter). The museum is closed on New Year's Day, Good Friday, the May Day bank holiday, Christmas Eve, Christmas Day and Boxing Day. The Old Royal Observatory is open for the same times. Admission charge. For further information telephone 01-858 4422.

How to get there

River buses run in summer from Westminster, Charing Cross and the Tower of London down the Thames to Greenwich Pier.

British Rail trains run from Cannon Street (not weekends), Charing Cross, Waterloo (East) and London Bridge stations to Maze Hill and Greenwich stations, which are only a few minutes walk from the museum. Buses passing near the museum are numbers 71, 177, 180, 185, 188 and 286. From July 1987 you can also travel to Greenwich via the regular service of the Docklands Light Railway to their Island Gardens station and then through the foot tunnel under the Thames. The DLR links into the Underground system at Tower Hill.

CUTTY SARK, GREENWICH PIER

The name *Cutty Sark* means 'short chemise' and you will see that this is what the figurehead is wearing. Built in 1869, the clipper was designed to be the fastest ship bringing the new season's tea from China — 107 days was her record, in 1871. The opening of the Suez Canal gave the advantage in speed to steamships so the *Cutty Sark* transferred to the Australian trade, carrying wool round the Horn to Europe.

On board you will realise that cargo space had priority in the design: we would find even the accommodation for officers intolerably cramped — the bosun, carpenter, sailmaker and apprentices were all packed into the afterdeck house, but at least they were on deck! Most daunting of all, though, is the prospect of handling the sails and complicated rigging supporting the three towering masts. Whatever the weather, the seamen had to be sure how to control the ropes — 10 miles (16 km) of them — which set 32,000 square feet (3000 sq m) of canvas sails.

Gipsy Moth IV stands nearby. She is the 18 ton ketch in which Sir Francis Chichester sailed around the world in 274 days in 1966-7 with only one stop, at Sydney. Moored a little further on is quite a different vessel, the Book Boat — a floating bookshop!

Admission
Cutty Sark and *Gipsy Moth IV* are open on Mondays to Saturdays from 11 a.m. to 6 p.m. and on Sundays from 2.30 p.m. to 6 p.m. but they close at 5 p.m. in winter. There is an admission charge for each vessel. Children must be accompanied by an adult. School parties can book ahead and gain a reduced rate: apply to The Master, Clipper Ship *Cutty Sark*, King William Walk, Greenwich, London SE10 9BG (telephone 01-858 3445).

How to get there
As for the National Maritime Museum.

THE THAMES BARRIER
Opened in 1984 the Thames Barrier has already been described as the 'eighth wonder of the modern world' and, with the curved stainless steel roofs of its piers, it is certainly an impressive sight. It was built to prevent the possibility of London being flooded yet still allow ships to use the river. A third of a mile (640 metres) wide, it has ten separate steel gates which block the river in the event of high tides. Each of the four main gates is as high as a five storey building while half a million tons of concrete was used to construct the piers and sills of the barrier. At the visitors' centre (for which there is an admission charge) you can see an audio-visual display about the Barrier; why it was necessary, how it was built and how it is operated. For further information, write to the Thames Barrier Centre, 1 Unity Way, Woolwich SE18 5NJ, or telephone 01-854 1373. Charlton and Woolwich Dockyard British Rail stations are both nearby and the 51, 96, 161, 177 and 180 buses go past the Centre. Alternatively you can take a river boat from either Westminster Pier (1¼ hours away) or Greenwich Pier (25 minutes away) — see chapter 3.

20. The Royal Air Force, Battle of Britain and Bomber Command Museums

When air pioneer Claude Graham White bought land at Hendon in 1911 for an airfield, he had no idea it was soon to be commandeered for war service, later to be the outstanding Royal Air Force air display centre and ultimately, in 1972, the home of the national museum of the Royal Air Force. Exceptionally well organised, it shows the history of the service in a series of galleries ranged along the side of the vast aircraft hall, a separate gallery for temporary exhibitions, a cinema and an art gallery. Across the car park the Battle of Britain is commemorated in its own museum; the Roundel restaurant is in the same building.

A vast new **Bomber Command Museum** has been built adjacent to the main building. It shows the development of bomber aircraft from the DH9A of the First World War to the awe-inspiring Vulcan, the V bomber similar to the type which took part in the Falklands campaign. Other aircraft on display include the Vickers Vimy, Wellington, Mosquito, Lancaster and the actual Valiant which dropped Britain's first megaton bomb. Full scale reconstructions of a USAAF Operations Room and Sir Barnes Wallis's study together with his remarkable creation, the bouncing bomb, are also featured.

The Royal Air Force Museum

The notice board to the left of the entrance hall gives the times and titles of films showing from 2.00 to 3.00 p.m. from Monday to Friday. Visit the galleries first: go upstairs to the left, past pictures of early efforts to get off the ground, to gallery 1 and the gentle balloons of 1870 manned by redcoated Royal Engineers of the Balloon Battalion. S. F. Cody, a pioneer in powered flight, invented the curious man lifting kite on display. He is also shown at the controls of the Nulli-Secundus airship.

In a glass case further on is a small piece of the Wright brothers' famous 'Flyer', which made the first powered flight in 1903 and inspired pioneers everywhere, such as J. T. C. Moore-Brabazon, who won the dynamically sculptured Michelin Trophy nearby. By 1914 aeroplanes were ready to begin their own chapter in the history of warfare and the army and navy both had flying sections. The dapper figure of a Royal Flying Corps flight sergeant enlivens the workshop scene in gallery 2; notice the delicacy of the structure and the robustness of the engines. Much of the aircraft hall can be seen from the viewing platform on the right.

The fragile machines suffered heavily in their new roles as fighters and bombers — see the diorama of a trench under air attack — and the constant repairs were done in tented hangars

60

like the one here. You will see how aircraft, equipment and weapons developed during the war: compare the anti-personnel 'flechettes' and the 1650 pound (750 kg) SN bomb, the 1914 and 1918 cockpits, and the change, in April 1918, from Royal Flying Corps to Royal Air Force. Do not miss the 'Very Gallant Gentleman', in a lovely leather flying coat, and the appearance of ladies, one even astride a motorcycle (next to the magnificent Crossley tender), the others in a nearby rather spartan WRAF hut.

Much of the immediate success of the new service was due to its first leader, Lord Trenchard, under whom it soon commanded great respect. It produced heroes in both wars who won the Victoria or George Cross and they are commemorated here.

Downstairs is displayed the work of the service between the wars. Peacekeeping abroad, airmen used armoured cars like the magnificent yellow Rolls-Royce here and were dressed, like the attendant airman, in long baggy shorts. The 'star-ship' cabin turns out to be the cabin of the redoubtable R33 airship. Nearby is the pressure suit worn by Sqn Ldr Swain to gain the world altitude record of 49,967 feet (15,229 metres) in 1936.

Information from the Chain Home radar towers modelled in gallery 8, and from the Royal Observer Corps operative, shown nearby, gave early warning of enemy attack. Word eventually reached fighter stations, like the one in the diorama with a Spitfire in the dispersal bay. To the right of the hall is the shop with its wide range of souvenirs.

Twenty years on, the WRAF ladies are not much more comfortable, but some are shown at work. Airmen shot down or captured were honour bound to get back home if they could and some did, helped by the ingenious aids provided by the RAF — this last section is full of adventure.

Galleries 10 and 11 show a radically different picture of jet aircraft and the sophisticated equipment of a modern armed service. Look at the great life-saving Martin-Baker ejection seat in gallery 10 and see the splendid audio-visual displays about the Royal Air Force of today in Gallery 11.

The Main Hall is the heart of the museum, just like an enormous hangar — in fact it is two 1915 hangars joined by a central section to make the museum. Some exhibits are unique and will be there most of the time, like the very early planes such as the splendid Bleriot XI Monoplane of 1911 and the biplane flying boat Supermarine Stranraer. Also on show are a Hudson aircraft, a Dornier 24 and two Sopwiths. In the centre, Hawker aircraft strikingly commemorate the designs of Sir Sidney Camm which include the P1127, the prototype of the Harrier.

The Battle of Britain Museum is devoted to the contest between the air forces of Britain and Germany between July and

October 1940 and shows clearly the impact of enemy attack on both the Royal Air Force and the people. The first tableau shows the grim remains of a Hurricane fighter, shot down on 31st August 1940 by two Messerschmitts, guarded by a civilian Local Defence Volunteer. One upstairs shows an Underground railway station used as an air raid shelter.

Of the magnificent collection of aeroplanes, some such as the Spitfire and Messerschmitts actually flew in the battle; all of them played important roles in the war. A dispersal pen shelters the Spitfire and a Hurricane and houses an exhibition gallery of war relics, amongst which you can find a smart stirrup pump, an air-raid siren, incendiary bombs, a Browning gun and a swastika panel taken from an aircraft as a trophy.

Upstairs the story of the battle is told in a series of display panels. All sorts of information about both air forces follows and there is always a good overhead view of the aeroplanes, particularly the magnificent Sunderland flying boat.

For details of the education service including introductory talks, trail sheets, project and book queries, and questionnaires, apply to the Education Officer, Royal Air Force Museum, Hendon, London NW9 5LL (telephone: 01-205 2266, ext 228).

Admission

The museums are open from 10 a.m. to 6 p.m. (Sundays 2 p.m. to 6 p.m.) and closed on Christmas Eve, Christmas Day, Boxing Day, New Year's Day, Good Friday and May Day. There is a large free car park and a souvenir shop. There is an admission charge for the Battle of Britain Museum and the Bomber Command Museum. For further information telephone 01-205 2266.

How to get there

The Northern Line underground station at Colindale is thirteen minutes walk away. The number 79 bus stop at the junction of Edgware Road and Colindale Avenue is about twenty-five minutes walk away. The museum is close to the A5, A41 and M1.

WEMBLEY STADIUM TOUR

Guided tours lasting just over an hour are now taken around Wembley Stadium. You can see the players' changing rooms kitted out for a match, walk up the players' tunnel, relax in the royal box and see the famous trophy cabinet. The tours start each day at 10 a.m., 11 a.m., 12 noon, 2 p.m., 3 p.m. (and 4 p.m. in summer). No tours on Christmas Day, Boxing Day, New Year's Day and the day of an event. Children under five are free. For further information telephone 01-903 4864.

21. The Bethnal Green Museum of Childhood

The Bethnal Green Museum of Childhood is a branch of the Victoria and Albert Museum. The collection of toys and dolls, one of the most important in the world, is displayed in three galleries.

The toys

The eye is caught by the carved, brightly painted wooden toys from Germany, where such traditional toys were first produced in quantity, and still are today. Noah's Arks, with their troops of animals, have been popular since the early nineteenth century and a small fleet of these is on display. Toy soldiers are on show in a big fort, and the railway enthusiast can see model trains by most of the well known makers. All sorts of toy forms of transport made of wood or metal, in all sizes, are in the collection. There are also toy theatres, including a large marionette theatre of the eighteenth century from Italy, and puppets of every kind and age. A large collection of board games, of teddy bears and other soft toys, all compete for attention with the optical toys, the automata, the model circus and the Action Man.

Dolls' houses

The Museum has a fine collection of dolls' houses. The earliest is the Nuremberg Dolls' House, made in 1673. It has a stocking stretcher on one wall, and a baby walker to keep the baby safe while the mother says her prayers by the four-poster bed.

One of the semi-educational toys is the Nuremberg kitchen, made in the eighteenth century — a box containing everything a little girl of that period would need to know; model kitchens such as this were used for instruction in German schools. Under the dresser is a hen-coop where hens were kept till they were needed for dinner. There is also a turning spit in front of the oven, and balancing scales hanging against the wall.

There is also a most realistic 1840 model of a butcher's shop, displaying all the cuts of meat and whole carcases, and the butcher himself standing at the door.

The dolls

The remarkable collection of dolls is arranged to show how dolls have developed since 1700. Perhaps the early stiff wooden dolls are not very cuddly but they are beautifully dressed.

Small girls find 'Princess Daisy' the star attraction. She is an English doll (with an elaborate Dutch layette), and was given to Queen Mary in 1899 for her own baby, Princess Mary. She has a pink satin and cream lace cradle, and her own pearl necklace with a real diamond clasp.

Upstairs is a fine collection of children's costume from about

1700 to the present day, along with nursery furniture and other relics of past childhoods. The big centre space of the building is usually taken up with a temporary exhibition. In the basement is the Art Room, open to young visitors on Saturdays.

Admission

Open weekdays (including Bank Holidays) except Friday 10 a.m. to 6 p.m., Sundays 2.30 p.m. to 6 p.m. Closed May Day Bank Holiday, Christmas Eve, Christmas Day, Boxing Day and New Year's Day. For information about activities for children in groups or as individuals in term and during holidays telephone 01-980 2415 or 01-589 6371 extension 382/429.

How to get there

The Museum of Childhood is in Cambridge Heath Road, E2. It is only five minutes' walk from Bethnal Green underground station (on the Central Line).

22. The Geffrye Museum

The Geffrye Museum is housed in the former almshouses of the Ironmongers' Company. Most of the collection of historic furniture and woodwork from 1600 to 1939 is effectively displayed in a series of period room settings begun by Marjorie Quennell when she was curator in 1935 and since improved and extended.

'Idleback'

The displays begin with the Georgian Street, which includes a fully equipped woodworker's shop. Off the long corridor open the room settings (with a library halfway down and a coffee shop behind) and beside each room are detailed descriptions of particular items. It is interesting to see the way living gradually became easier. The open hearth kitchen is fascinating — the large iron implements and utensils are beautifully devised — look for the 'idleback' to help tip a very hot kettle and the toasting forks.

The highly carved Elizabethan chairs and chests and the simple elegant eighteenth-century furniture are very attractive but nineteenth-century furniture looks more inviting to sit on! The Victorians obviously loved lots of ornaments, like the dried flowers under glass. In the Voysey room there is a cylinder phonograph and an early telephone. Although the plain, uncarved furniture in the 1930s rooms looks old-fashioned yet familiar, items like the wireless and television sets seem very quaint!

On Saturdays worksheets and puzzles linked to the collection are available. It is essential to book group visits.

64

Admission

The museum is open on weekdays except Mondays (unless a Bank Holiday) 10 a.m. to 5 p.m. and on Sundays 2 p.m. to 5 p.m. It is closed on Christmas Day, Boxing Day and New Year's Day. There are a museum shop and a tea and coffee bar. The museum telephone number is 01-739 9893.

How to get there

The Geffrye Museum is in Kingsland Road, Shoreditch, E2, twenty minutes walk from Liverpool Street (left) or Old Street (right then left at junction) underground stations. Buses 22, 22A, 48, 67, 97, 149 and 243 stop at the museum.

23. The Science Museum

Children visiting the Science Museum should make a bee-line for the **Children's Gallery,** in the *rear* part of the basement. There are two entrances: one near the locomotives and old cars, the other by the fire engines.

As well as dioramas showing the development of transport, from a man carrying game on his back perhaps ten thousand years ago, and pack horses and a single-masted ship of 1400 to a modern motorway, there are countless push-button working models of various delights from waterwheels to a teleprinter and a baffling optical illusion.

Many of the models and exhibits actually work, including engines of all kinds and a periscope from HMS *Tiptoe* (1945) that gives a view of both the ground floor and the first floor. It emerges near a diesel-electric locomotive and (on the wall) a blue and gold clock, an exact (though smaller) replica of the famous astronomical clock at Hampton Court. It tells the hour, the day of the month, the month itself, the number of days since the beginning of the year, and the phases of the moon.

By the entrance from Exhibition Road, you will find **Launch Pad,** the exciting 'hands-on' technology exhibition. Most of the exhibits can be operated to demonstrate how basic scientific principles, such as sound, energy and reflection work. There is a water generator where you can raise water and release it on to a waterwheel which powers an electric light; or you can pedal hard on a fixed bicycle to see how many connected lights your energy can illuminate. There are simple robots to be worked, distorted images of yourself on television and a mirror which convinces you that you can shake your own hand!

The Rocket and Puffing Billy

Out in the Centre Hall you find the Transport exhibits, one of the most famous of which is George Stephenson's *Rocket* locomotive constructed in 1829 — and in the possession of the museum since 1863. The *Rocket* was built to compete for a premium of £500 for a loco capable of hauling a specified load at 10 mph. Only the *Rocket* completed the course, running 35 miles at an average speed of 14 mph.

Puffing Billy, the oldest locomotive in the world, constructed in 1813, is here, and nearby is the Great Western *Caerphilly Castle*, a 1923 loco, which travelled nearly two million miles before being withdrawn from service in 1960. A platform has been built alongside, so that visitors may look into the cab.

Amongst this splendour of the past is a York to London Royal Mail coach of 1827 (up to 1784 the mail had been carried on horseback by postboys). And there are old motor-cars and trams.

Near the escalator is an impressive automated diorama showing a team on a cold dark North Sea rig, drilling for gas, part of the story of gas from ancient China to the present.

It is a small step for you, but a giant leap in technology, as you go to the Space Exploration gallery nearby. This has at its centre the actual Apollo 10 space capsule which first circled the moon in 1969. This was a preparation for the moon landing two months later, which is reconstructed opposite with a replica of the Apollo 11 capsule on a lunar landscape and wax figures of Neil Armstrong and Buzz Aldrin.

The Tonbridge Telegraph Office

On the first floor is a gallery devoted to the history of telecommunications. The telegraph was the first widespread system and here you can see a reproduction of the Tonbridge telegraph office as it was in the 1850s. Also on display are the Telstar satellite, the radio consoles of a Lancaster bomber and a ship's radio cabin, massive underwater cables and a clutch of optical fibres which will pass through the eye of a needle.

The first powered flight

An escalator leads up to the **Aernonautics Gallery** on the third floor, where two of the star attractions are a Battle of Britain Spitfire — P9444 — and a Hurricane — L1592. Almost as popular is a replica of the Wright Flyer, in which two American brothers, Orville and Wilbur Wright, made the first successful flight (in 1903) in a powered aeroplane. The flight lasted only twelve seconds.

One of the reasons the Wright brothers turned to powered flight was the death after a crash of a much-respected glider designer and pilot, Otto Lilienthal. He produced a series of gliders between 1891 and 1896, and made over two thousand short flights. One of his gliders is strung from the ceiling in this gallery, showing how his body was strapped between the wings, leaving his arms free. This glider has bamboo longitudinal members, willow wing ribs hinged to the centre section of the frame, and fabric wings shaped like a bird's.

Among the other exhibits is the nose portion of a Gloster Meteor F3 (the plane from which the first ejection of a man in a parachute took place in July 1946), the Cody biplane of 1912, a rocket engine, and many models, including one of the Anglo-French supersonic transport Concorde, which made its maiden flight in March 1970. In the same display case is a model of a Voisin biplane, which made the first cross-country flight in Britain, in 1908 — at 34 mph.

Prisoner-of-war models

On the half floor below the planes are model sailing ships of all kinds, including luggers, oyster smacks, a seven-masted schooner, dhows, and a lightship. Near them are model steam ships, including the *Great Eastern,* the largest vessel afloat from 1858 to 1899. There is a model of the 83,673-ton *Queen Elizabeth,* an 1824 figurehead from HMS *North Sea,* and a case full of models made by French prisoners of war between 1793 and 1815, when they were interned at Dartmoor, Portchester Castle and Norman Cross. These little ships were made of wood or bone, chiefly ivory, and are highly prized though not strictly accurate. The pride of the collection is *The Prince* (1670)—possibly the finest ship model of its period in existence. This was once the flagship of the Duke of York (later James II). It was designed by the great Phineas Pett, who had operated as a privateer off the Barbary Coast.

Admission

Open on weekdays 10 a.m. to 6 p.m. and on Sundays 2.30 p.m. to 6 p.m. Closed on Christmas Eve, Christmas Day, Boxing Day, New Year's Day, May Day Monday and Good Friday.

School parties are welcome, but teachers or parents acting as escorts are advised to make a preliminary visit, or to write in, to make sure that a gallery or exhibit of particular interest is available for inspection.

Special demonstration-lectures can be arranged to suit the needs and interests of any group of children from ten-year-olds upwards.

Requests for demonstration-lectures and tickets for special lectures should be sent to The Director, Education Department, The Science Museum, South Kensington, London, SW7 2DD (telephone 01-589 3456).

How to get there

The museum is only a few minutes' walk from South Kensington underground station, and buses passing near include numbers 14, 30, 74 and 97.

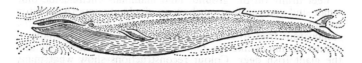

24. The Natural History Museum

The public galleries of the Natural History Museum are undergoing major changes. If you plan to visit a particular gallery or exhibit it would be wise to telephone the Museum to check that it is open or on show.

A popular exhibition, **Dinosaurs and their Living Relatives,** is on show in the Central Hall. It includes spectacular fossil skeletons, including the 84 foot (25 m) *Diplodocus,* the horned *Triceratops* and the armour-plated *Scolosaurus.* Also on view is a skull of the meat-eating *Tyrannosaurus rex.* There are scaled-down glass-fibre models showing what the dinosaurs would have looked like in the flesh and a series of display cases which explain how dinosaurs are related to living animals.

In the North Hall, nearby, look for the fish which surprised everyone when one was caught in the waters of Madagascar in 1938. The coelacanth was thought to have been extinct for ninety million years. A few yards away stands Chi-Chi, the giant panda from London Zoo, stuffed after her death in 1972.

Cells and organs

The **Hall of Human Biology** is reached from the Bird Gallery on the ground floor and is in ten sections (really too much to take in on one visit). Each section has a theme, such as growing, and is illustrated by diagrams, models, slide shows, cartoons, games to play, mechanisms to manipulate. Huge cross sections of cells and organs display their amazing complexity. You move your own muscles to manipulate devices showing how muscles work. Your reactions to emergency situations show how the hormones carry messages for your protection. You can discover that you have three types of memory, how to distinguish between them and how you learn. There is even a video game called 'Imposters' which teaches you about human genetics. After an energetic tour you will have discovered quite a lot about yourself.

Discovering Mammals

Dominating this new exhibition is the famous 90 foot (27 m) model of a blue whale. On the balcony are fascinating sea mammals with exhibits showing how they live, the great distances they travel, how they communicate and the problems of conservation.

Feet firmly on the ground, land mammals encircle the blue whale and you can find out how an elephant supports its 6 ton weight and what has happened to the forest where the rhinocerous tries to survive. Bizarre fossils show the shape of extinct mammals like the famous mammoths from Siberia and the giant Irish deer. Colour reconstructions show what many extinct animals probably looked like. On videos you can see film of underwater mammals and on one of the interactive exhibits you can match your intelligence with that of a dolphin.

The dead dodo

Birds are shown in a long gallery immediately to the left of the main entrance. The favourite is undoubtedly the dodo, from Mauritius—extinct and 'as dead as the dodo' since 1693. Amongst the other exhibits is a case showing different kinds of birds' nests. Two of the most interesting are the Indian tailor bird's, which neatly stitches two long leaves together to hold the nest, and the baya weaver bird's extraordinary tubular woven nest. Look for the smallest bird in the world, the bee humming bird, which is about the size of a bumblebee.

British birds are grouped together in their own pavilion, with a domed roof representing the sky. Across this goes a flight of mallard, in formation, and on a lonely pinnacle of rock sits a golden eagle.

The **Ecology Exhibition** on the ground floor takes as its theme an oak woodland and a rocky shore and shows how plants and animals interact with each other and their surroundings. It includes lots of specimens, interactive machines and dioramas.

British Natural History

If you enjoy country walks, and want help in identifying the different plants and animals you spot, this exhibition on the top floor should help you. It shows examples of over 2,000 species of flora and fauna that can be found in the seven main habitats of the British Isles.

There is also an awe-inspiring display of minerals and meteorites, and there are galleries of mammals, insects, fossils and botanical specimens.

The Family Centre

The Family Centre is open during the Easter and summer

school holidays from 10.30 a.m. to 12.30 p.m. and again from 2 p.m. to 4 p.m. each day except Saturday. There are numerous activities for children and their parents, including nature quizzes and looking through microscopes. There are also natural history specimens, such as bones and fossils to examine at close quarters.

Admission
Open Mondays to Saturdays 10 a.m. to 6 p.m., Sundays 2.30 p.m. to 6 p.m. The museum is closed on Christmas Eve, Christmas Day, Boxing Day, Good Friday, New Year's Day and May Day holiday. Admission charge. There is a snack bar on the ground floor and a cafeteria on the first. The museum's telephone number if 01-589 6323.

How to get there
The nearest undergound station is South Kensington. Buses to take are 14, 30, 45 and 74.

25. The Victoria and Albert Museum

This museum specialises in fine and applied art of all countries, styles and periods. There is so much to see that it is best to select particular exhibits that interest you. For example, most people want to see the Costume Court and Tipu's Tiger.

From the main entrance go through Room 49 and turn left, walking through Oriental galleries — see if you can find the beautiful Javanese shadow puppet and a Tibetan cousin to a guitar — until you come to Tipu's Tiger in Room 41.

Tipu's is a wooden tiger. He is mauling a startled-looking man who has somehow managed to keep his hat on. The animal contains a miniature mechanised organ which, when operated by a push-button, gives out the cry of the mauled man. It is not very convincing, but a bit scary to the very young. The tiger was probably made in Mysore about 1795.

The Dress Collection

This museum has some of the finest period clothes in the world. Look especially for the doublet and hose said to have been worn by James I before he became king in 1603 — the plum-coloured velvet is topped by a large stiff white collar which stands out like a huge pie frill! See how fine and ornate some of the court dresses were and how difficult to wear. There are period dolls, too, with sets of tiny corsets, slippers and mittens, for every occasion.

The 'giraffe piano'

Upstairs from the Dress Collection is the Musical Instruments Gallery. Probably the most curious exhibit is the 'giraffe piano', equipped with drum and bells, looking like an upturned grand piano. A beautifully carved violin is said to have belonged to Charles II.

Look into the gallery opposite the Dress Collection to find out what artists such as Leonardo and here, Raphael, meant by 'cartoon'. These Raphael Cartoons, huge as they are, were painted in 1515 as designs for tapestries for the Sistine Chapel in Rome. Charles I, then Prince of Wales, bought them in 1623, Queen Victoria lent them to the museum in 1865 and here they have remained.

The Great Bed of Ware

The Great Bed of Ware is in Room 54. This huge oak bed, made in England about 1580, is large enough to hold four couples. It is decorated at the bedhead with carvings of bearded men. The bed was once installed in an inn and (by custom) all those who slept in it carved their initials on it. It is mentioned by Sir Toby Belch in *Twelfth Night*.

Nearby is a small, brightly painted keyboard instrument — the virginals that actually belonged to Queen Elizabeth I, who was an excellent musician.

Royal relics

In Room 53, devoted to English embroidery between 1540 and 1640, is a military scarf said to have been worn by Charles I at the battle of Edgehill in 1642. The upholstered chair in this room, now faded but once bright red, is believed to have been used by the king at his trial in Westminster Hall.

There is another royal relic in Room 54 — part of the hangings known as the Oxburgh Hangings, which were made by Mary, Queen of Scots, and Bess of Hardwick, Countess of Shrewsbury, about 1570, during the queen's captivity.

Arms and armour

The Victoria and Albert's examples of European arms and armour (in Rooms 88a and 90) have been selected specially to show the various techniques of ornament applied to swords, firearms, helmets, rapiers, daggers, breast plates and shields.

There are wheel-lock guns inlaid with engraved staghorn; a 1520 steel horse's head defence engraved with a crowned Polish eagle; flint-lock pistols with engraved and gilded mounts, and an air-gun said to have belonged to George II.

The Pusey Horn legend

While on this floor, walk through the silver display in the corridor numbered (as you go from the Armoury) 69 to 65. This collection of Continental and English domestic silver is the finest in the world.

Amongst all the magnificence is the Pusey Horn (fifteenth century) to which is attached a legend dating back to Canute. There are many instances of odd land tenures in England. One such was said to concern Pusey in Oxfordshire. According to legend, Canute gave William Pusey the manor, and presented him with the Pusey Horn as a token of ownership. The horn is of ox or buffalo, mounted near the centre with a silver gilt band. It stands on two skinny legs attached to the band. In James II's reign, the manor was recovered in a lawsuit, over which presided Judge Jeffreys, by the production of the Pusey Horn.

Admission

Open weekdays (except Fridays) 10 a.m. to 5.50 p.m., Sundays 2.30 p.m. to 5.50 p.m. The museum is closed on Christmas Eve, Christmas Day, Boxing Day, New Year's Day, Good Friday and May Day. For further information telephone 01-589 6371.

How to get there

The museum entrance is in Cromwell Road. Buses 14, 30 and 74 stop outside. The nearest underground station is South Kensington.

26. The National Army Museum

The National Army Museum is in Royal Hospital Road, near the home of the 'Chelsea Pensioners'. The exterior is very impressive and the entrance hall offers a glittering welcome. Look at the delicate model soldiers in the case on the left.

A ramp to the right leads down past the banners and guidons (double-pointed flags) of famous regiments to the **Arms and the Army Exhibition,** a perfect demonstration of the use and development of firearms from early muskets to automatic weapons, and of edged weapons from the pike and broadsword to the bayonet and modern cavalry sword. Each section is illustrated by weapons and explanatory notes, often with background enlargements of contemporary pictures which show the weapons in use. There are models showing how firearms work and how they were made.

Siege money

Return up the ramp and go up the staircase to the right to the **Story of the Army 1485-1914.** (On the right, note the guidon of the 3rd Bengal Irregular Cavalry and the strange spelling of Kabul.) The army begins its history from the formation of the Yeomen of the Guard by Henry VII (case 1 to the right), but it was the success of the Puritan New Model Army in the Civil War which proved the advantage of a regular disciplined army. Notice in case 7 the unique square siege money used in the siege of Newark and the 'iron secrets' in case 12. By 1719 there were 72,000 men under arms to fight under Marlborough against the French and soon after against the Stuart pretenders. The Scottish targe (shield) in case 20 shows how vulnerable the Scots were thirty years later at Culloden.

The skeleton of Napoleon's charger

The most stirring exhibits are those belonging to national heroes, especially those who died in battle, like the sash of General Wolfe and the faded cloak in which he was wrapped at his death after the successful storming of Quebec (28). Sir John Moore's sash, worn when he died at Corunna (43), and the handkerchief and glove of the Earl of Uxbridge, stained with blood when his leg was amputated at Waterloo — and the saw which was used (44) — are sombre relics of the wars against Napoleon, amidst which the skeleton of the Emperor's favourite charger, Marengo, seems rather pathetic. In case 51 is the telescope of Lord Raglan, through which perhaps he saw the disaster of the Charge of the Light Brigade, and the cloak of Captain Nolan, who carried the fatally wrong order which began it. Florence Nightingale, who nursed the dreadful casualties of the Crimean War, was called 'the lady with the lamp'. She carried a candle lantern like the one in case 70.

Rorke's Drift

Look for the examples of the cartridges which were the final cause of the Indian Mutiny (52) and the photographic story of the British army in Afghanistan (56). Would you have known that the Sikh quoits in case 58 were throwing knives? In 73b is the 'volume which saved his life' belonging to General Wolseley. Further on is a model of Rorke's Drift where, in 1879, 140 British soldiers held off four thousand Zulus. The gallery ends with the Boer War. Baden-Powell's slouch hat is here, as well as the telegram instruction to mobilise the army, received at 5 p.m. on 4th August 1914.

A new gallery concentrates on the armies of the two world wars up to the professional army of today. This is **Flanders to the Falklands 1914-82.** Notable exhibits include specially commissioned dioramas of the first full-scale tank attack at Cambrai (1917) and the Normandy invasion (1944), and reconstructions of a typical trench on the Western Front (1916), a National Service barrack room of the 1950s and a captured Argentine position on Mount Tumbledown in the Falklands (1982). Free-standing exhibits include a bren-gun carrier in desert-war camouflage. Here too you can see the Victoria Cross won by Lt Col H. Jones of the 2nd Parachute Battalion who was killed in the Falklands.

You go up to the **Art Gallery** and the **Uniform Gallery** past pictures of battles all over the world; one of them is an enormous canvas of the battle of Ulundi against the Zulus in 1879. The **Uniform Gallery** displays a multitude of medals and decorations, including the decorations of the late Duke of Windsor, formerly Edward VIII. The collars and badges of the orders of chivalry, like the Garter and the Thistle, are beautifully made. Along the right-hand wall are cases similarly devoted to great generals.

Army dress progressed slowly from the colourful but cumbersome uniforms and headdresses of the seventeenth and eighteenth centuries to the unexciting but practical khaki of the twentieth. Horses were once beautifully accoutred — see the shabraques in cases 3 and 4 for example. Look for the comfortable campbed for a nineteenth-century officer, and the wooden serpent and the ophicleide (16). Bandsmen do not often carry them these days! And finally, note the difference between a bearskin and a busby (19).

For details of the broadly based education service, which includes illustrated topic and general worksheets for primary and secondary pupils and lectures for sixth forms, and of the Holiday Club, which functions in the summer holidays for children over seven, write to the Education Department, National Army Museum, Royal Hospital Road, London SW3 4HT (telephone: 01-730 0717, ext 28).

Admission
Open daily 10 a.m. to 5.30 p.m.; Sundays 2 p.m. to 5.30 p.m. Closed Christmas Eve, Christmas Day, Boxing Day, New Year's Day, Good Friday and May Day. Admission free. Telephone 01-730 0701, ext 49.

How to get there
The nearest underground station is Sloane Square, fifteen minutes' walk away. The 11, 19, and 22 buses go along King's Road (stop at Smith Street), the 137 stops at the junction with Royal Hospital Road, and the 39 runs an irregular service past the door.

27. The London Toy and Model Museum

The London Toy and Model Museum originally occupied the two lower floors of a restored Victorian house in Queensway but in 1984 the exhibition was greatly increased by the acquisition of the adjoining property. A wide range of toys dating from the middle of the nineteenth century to the present day are on display.

Stanley Baldwin's clockwork pig

As you enter go down to the museum's lower floor where several permament exhibitions have been set up. The Nursery is a collection of young children's toys — rocking horses, dolls, cuddly animals and especially teddy bears. Find out how these got their name from Theodore Roosevelt and look for the clockwork suede pig which was given to Stanley Baldwin in 1872.

Girls will probably be most interested in a five-storey Victorian dolls' house. The living quarters of servants, children and parents are reconstructed in great detail. Look for the old warming pan, the miniature piece of sheet music on the piano and the outsized box of matches. The walls in one of the corridors are even being wallpapered.

The lower floor also has a display of the shop fronts of two of Britain's most famous toy companies, Basset-Lowke and Meccano Ltd. By pressing buttons the wheels of a large model of the Royal Scot can be operated in the Basset-Lowke window, as can a Meccano roundabout in the other shop. Also on this floor are the Tiatsa Collection, of over 15,000 model cars, and dolls dating from the mid eighteenth century.

Penny toys

Returning to the ground floor, the second gallery you will find is the Tin Toy Room which houses the Museum's collection of toy boats, cars (including a toy of the first self-propelled road vehicle), fire engines and buses. Outside the Tin Toy Room is the Penny Toy Showcase with a large collection of penny toys. These were manufactured between 1895 and 1914 and were wisely aimed at the meagre purses of the children of those days. Most of those on display here are tinplate. Try to find the various trademarks of J. Ph. Meier who has painted on the majority of them either a dog and a cart, 'J Ph M', 'J P M', 'JM' or simply 'M'.

Model railway systems

The Train Room is at the end of your tour and opens up on to the garden railway systems. There are numerous shelves of model locomotives of all nationalities. Look for the various oddities and the strange uses to which these toys were put in the past, like C. Rowley's 1847 cigar holder, the oldest train in the collection, or an 1853 inkwell — an interesting contrast to today's kind! A OO working railway depicting a country branch line is displayed above a typical tinplate terminus based loosely on Leipzig Station in the 1930s.

Special exhibitions are organised and visitors can find out what these will be by telephoning 01-262 7905. A 2½ inch (64 mm) gauge railway runs in a large garden which the museum has retained. There are also gauge 1 and O railways, as well as one you can ride on, a children's roundabout and a pond for model boats.

Admission

Open Tuesdays to Saturdays 10 a.m. to 5.30 p.m., Sundays 11 a.m. to 5.30 p.m. Closed every Monday except Bank Holiday Mondays. Closed Christmas Day and New Year's Day. Admission charge. Light refreshments are available in the cafe overlooking the boating pond and the museum shop stocks a wide selection of books on toys, as well as souvenirs and postcards. Telephone: 01-262 7905 or 9450.

How to get there

The museum is at 21-23 Craven Hill, W2, five minutes walk from Lancaster Gate, Queensway or Bayswater underground stations. Alternatively catch any bus on the Bayswater Road between Notting Hill Gate and Marble Arch and ask for the Leinster Terrace stop.

Hamley's of Regent Street, the largest toy shop in the world, began its life as long ago as 1760 under the name of 'Noah's Ark' in High Holborn. Its policy was 'only the best for the best', something at which it still aims after numerous changes of sites, a couple of fires and an unforeseeable expansion. Whether you buy anything or not, there is always something to watch on the shop's six floors — card tricks, jokes, magicians, train sets in action, all sorts of remote-controlled models. Every conceivable kind of toy is available, from soft toys and doll's houses for the very young to golf clubs and snooker tables for teenagers and adults. A new department is open now housing a selection of electronic games and home computers. The shop's telephone number is 01-734 3161. Its address is 188-196 Regent Street, near Oxford Circus.

28. The National Gallery

The National Gallery was opened in 1824 and was centred around the private collections of Sir George Beaumont and John Julius Angerstein. Although there were only thirty-eight paintings twenty-four thousand people visited the Gallery in the first seven months. Now, with a collection of over two thousand pictures, almost three million visitors come each year.

It would take a day to walk around the whole of the Gallery, but children will probably prefer to see the most famous and interesting pictures, like Rembrandt's 'Belshazzar's Feast' in Room 26 or Henri Rousseau's colourful 'Tropical Storm with a Tiger' with its unreal appearance that makes it look like a scene from a dream, in Room 45. In Room 34 you can see several of Canaletto's views of Venice, drawn with such precision that on one a small coat of arms is recognisable as that of a particular Doge. The image which most people have of the Duke of Wellington comes from the painting by Goya in Room 42 and in Room 22a there is a picture of 'A Grotesque Old Woman' wearing a youthful dress and holding a budding rose! The magnificent Barry Rooms have been redecorated and house British paintings. Other artists with works on display in the Gallery include Picasso, Turner, Leonardo, Raphael, Michelangelo and Hogarth.

The Gallery organises various free activities to interest children. There are illustrated worksheets on themes common to many of the paintings, each of which takes about an hour to complete and is designed to be used in context with specific pictures. They can be obtained from the Children's Quiz desk at the Orange Street entrance during the holidays and from the Information Desk at other times. School parties can book Gallery talks and quizzes and the guided tours and talks are available to children. For further information telephone the Education Department on 01-839 3321 extension 290.

Admission
Open Mondays to Saturdays 10 a.m. to 6 p.m., Sundays 2 p.m. to 6 p.m. Closed from 24th to 26th December and New Year's Day. There is a restaurant on the lower floor. Admission free.

How to get there
Take the Underground to Charing Cross station and the Gallery is a few hundred yards away in Trafalgar Square.

29. The National Portrait Gallery

Just around the corner from the National Gallery, in St Martin's Place, you can see pictures of many of Britain's historical figures in the National Portrait Gallery. It is interesting to see what some of the world's greatest writers looked like. The portrait of William Shakespeare by an unknown artist was the first to enter the Gallery's collection and is the only picture with any claim to represent the Bard. Charles Dickens is shown beardless at twenty-six, and A. A. Milne with Christopher Robin and Pooh Bear.

Other figures here are Samuel Pepys, holding the music to one of his own songs, Lord Nelson and Lady Hamilton, whose relationship became one of Britain's most famous romances, and Sir Winston Churchill painted in a hazy 'snapshot' picture. British royalty is traced through the ages and the changes over the centuries in portraying the country's rulers are remarkable. Compare the paintings of the royal families of George V and George VI, the first filled with grandeur and formality, the other set in everyday clothes around a tea-table with the present Queen Mother pouring. You can also see the first portrait of the Princess of Wales, dressed in trousers and an open-necked blouse. This was slashed when first put on display, but has now been restored.

Admission

Open Mondays to Fridays 10 a.m. to 5 p.m., Saturdays 10 a.m. to 6 p.m., Sundays 2 p.m. to 6 p.m. Closed on Christmas Eve, Christmas Day, Boxing Day, New Year's Day, Good Friday and May Day. The Gallery's telephone number is 01-930 1552. The shop sells books and postcards about paintings. The Education Department has details of holiday activities. Admission free.

How to get there

As for the National Gallery.

Trafalgar Square at dusk is filled with spiralling and wheeling flocks of starlings which are a feature of 'London by night'.

Starlings feeding in the suburbs gather in small groups towards sundown, and the small groups join up with larger and larger groups until, in flocks of thousands strong, they fly off to their habitual roosts in London. The birds fly along set 'flight lines' and settle in dense concentrations around Trafalgar Square and St Paul's Cathedral.

30. The British Museum and British Library

The British Museum is one of the greatest treasure-houses in the world. It owes its beginning to Sir Hans Sloane, an Irishman who was born in 1660, the year Charles II was restored to the throne.

As a young man, Sloane studied botany, chemistry and anatomy, and later became the first physician to be made a hereditary baronet. He was one of the doctors who certified 'Queen Anne's dead!' in 1714.

Sloane had many scientific interests. He was president of the Royal Society in succession to Sir Isaac Newton, and had a fine collection of antiques, botanical specimens (some collected in Jamaica), gems and curiosities. He also had a library of more than fifty thousand books and four thousand manuscripts.

Only fifteen people at a time!

Sir Hans' valuable collection (offered for the low sum of £20,000), plus the presentation of the Royal Library of George III, persuaded Parliament to run a national lottery to raise funds to buy the Sloane collection and to administer a museum. A house was bought in Bloomsbury and the British Museum was opened in 1759 — to fifteen people at a time, three days a week. As the musuem grew the building was added to and rebuilt. There is so much to see that the problem is where to begin. A map of the different galleries is helpful and may be obtained from the Information Desk in the main entrance. There are children's trails for most parts of the museum and holiday events are organised. Telephone 01-636 1555, extension 511 for details.

Past the bookstall is the **Egyptian Sculpture Gallery**, where there are statues of kings and gods with heads of animals and birds, and a massive granite arm which probably came from a statue of Egypt's greatest king, Thothmoses III, who died about 1500 BC. His head is in the Egyptian Sculpture Gallery. (On the Embankment is a 68 foot (21 m) monolith known as Cleopatra's Needle. This obelisk — which has no connection with Cleopatra — was erected by Thothmoses, and towed to England in a cylinder in Queen Victoria's reign.)

Before you explore the Egyptian Sculpture Gallery you might like to detour to the **Assyrian Saloon**. The entrance — on the immediate left as you walk towards the Egyptian exhibits — is guarded by two winged, human-headed monsters. Round the walls are acutely observed and vividly sculptured panels that once covered the walls of the palace of Assyrian kings. Some of the panels show a king in his chariot hunting lions. Other scenes show the Assyrian army besieging walled cities, using battering rams on wheels that look very much like modern tanks. Downstairs are glass cases showing some of the actual breastplates, shields, helmets and swords used in these battles. The stairway leads from the Assyrian Saloon, near a triumphant procession returning from a hunt with dead lions, birds and a hare.

Broken by a madman

The Assyrian exhibits lead to two more winged monsters, each weighing about seven tons, and to a sort of 'crossroads'. Directly in front is a Roman mosaic laid in France in the second century AD. Looking down at the mosaic is the crouching Aphrodite, sculpted about 250 BC, lent to the museum by the Queen. Straight ahead is a statue of Apollo playing a lute. In the rooms behind him are early Roman wall paintings, some from Pompeii, jewellery, and the **Portland Vase.** This lovely vase is made of two layers of glass: white on dark blue, the white being cut away like a cameo to show the design in relief. The vase is now made up of fragments. It was broken by a madman in 1845, but skilfully put together again.

If you turn left at the Roman mosaic pavement, you walk through to the Duveen Gallery, where the **Elgin Marbles** are displayed. These friezes and statues from the Parthenon in Athens are called after Lord Elgin, who collected them in Athens in 1801-3. He brought them to England, and sold them to the government for £35,000, about half what they cost him to collect and ship. You can hire a half-hour sound guide about the Elgin Marbles, which are amongst the greatest sculptures of the world. Most of them were carved between 447 and 432 BC, and show vigorous riders and horses, bulls, and girls with sacrificial vessels. Upstairs are exhibitions about the Celts, Roman Britain and the Sutton Hoo Ship Burial from Suffolk.

The **Clock Room** is well worth a visit. Outstanding here are a large fourteenth century iron clock — still clicking away the minutes — and a carillon clock made in 1598 by Nicholas Vallin, clockmaker to Elizabeth I.

Mummies of cats and kittens

Returning to the Egyptian Sculpture Gallery, a staircase at the left-hand end (lined with framed mosaics of horses, fish, sea creatures and hunting scenes) leads to the **Second Egyptian Room.** Here are Egyptian mummies and their intricately carved mummy cases. Among them is the body of a pre-dynastic man (with hair breaking through his cracked skin) who died some 3,500 years before the birth of Christ. His body was preserved by the hot sands of Egypt under which he was buried and he is lying just as he was found. At the museum he is known as 'Ginger'.

Leading out of the Second Egyptian Room is the **First Egyptian Room,** where there are various bodies showing the great skill and care taken in wrapping them in bandages after death. There are also mummies of cats and kittens, a gazelle, a jackal and a dog.

A hungry hippopotamus

On the walls of the First Egyptian Room are paintings copied exactly from the Egyptian tombs. One picture shows a man being judged after death. His heart (which the Egyptians equated with the soul) is being weighed on a pair of scales and balanced against a feather, the symbol of truth and justice. Nearby stands a hippopotamus, eager to eat the man if he fails the test. (If he passes he will live 'happily ever after' in the beautiful Land of the West.)

THE BRITISH LIBRARY

As you come out of the Second Egyptian Room turn left and walk through the Room of Writing (on stone) to the staircase guarded by a three-storey high 'top-hatted' totem pole from British Columbia. At the foot of the staircase turn into the British Library galleries, the first of which houses the stamp collection, where there are cabinets holding stamps from all over the world.

The stamp collection leads to the **King's Library,** another of the museum's great treasures. Here thousands of books, many of them unique, are kept, including Caxton's *Aesop's Fables,* printed in Westminster in 1484, the first folio of *Mr William Shakespeare's Comedies, Histories and Tragedies,* printed in London in 1623, and the Gutenberg 42-lines-to-the-page Bible, the first substantial book printed in movable type.

Scott's last message

Straight ahead is the **Manuscript Saloon,** where there are letters and documents written by famous people, including the diary of Scott of the Antarctic, showing the page on which his last poignant message was written in pencil: 'For God's sake look after our people'. There is an essay written by Edward VI showing corrections made by his tutor; the original manuscript of *Alice's Adventures Under Ground* (as *Alice in Wonderland* was first called by Lewis Carroll) with illustrations by the author; and a letter from Nelson to his 'dearest Emma', Lady Hamilton, written two days before the battle of Trafalgar. Here, too, there is always someone looking at a copy of Magna Carta.

The British Museum often changes its exhibits, so visitors wanting to see something in particular should make enquiries first. There is a recorded information service on 01-580 1788.

Admission

Open Mondays to Saturdays 10 a.m. to 5 p.m., Sundays 2.30

p.m. to 6 p.m. The museum is not open on Christmas Eve, Christmas Day, Boxing Day, Good Friday, or the first Monday in May.

How to get there
   The nearest underground stations are Tottenham Court Road and Holborn (Kingsway). Useful buses include numbers 8, 14, 24, 25, 29 and 38.

31. Pollock's Toy Theatre and Toy Museum

Pollock's Toy Theatre and Toy Museum at Number 1 Scala Street occupies two little houses joined together.

   The founder was Benjamin Pollock, who married the daughter of John Redington, a printer of play books — containing the script, characters and scenery for toy theatre plays. The toy theatre was something more than a toy, being a real theatre in miniature, with all its plays adapted from real productions that had been staged in London theatres.

   In 1873 Pollock took over his father-in-law's business in Hoxton. He did all the prints himself, and when his two daughters grew up they painted those set aside for painting. It was these plain and tinted prints that inspired Robert Louis Stevenson's famous description: 'Penny plain and tuppence coloured'. Mr Green, originator of toy theatre, is asleep in his print shop whilst Pollock's daughter colours the sheets by hand with the aid of stencils.

   Pollock's incorporates a toy shop. Downstairs you can buy calico prints featuring 'Little Liz' dolls (in mop caps). Round about are various theatres already assembled. Up the stairways are framed old jigsaw puzzles and jumping-jacks, shabby puppets, a tiny grocer's shop with far-too-large miniature cans of Huntley and Palmer's ginger nuts and Bird's custard, and dozens of the dolls that Victorian children loved.

   The dolls may appeal most to the girls, but boys share their enthusiasm for toy theatres. More and more are sold every year, and boys who do buy them are following in famous footsteps, as Sir Winston Churchill had one as a boy.

Admission
   Open every weekday 10 a.m. to 5 p.m. Admission charge. School parties by arrangement. Telephone 01-636 3452 for details.

How to get there
   Pollock's Toy Museum is just off Tottenham Court Road, at the back of Goodge Street underground station. Buses going near include numbers 14, 24 and 73.

32. Madame Tussaud's

Everybody enjoys Madame Tussaud's, in Marylebone Road, and the possibility of staring intently at a wax figure who turns out to be real, or vice versa. There are usually about 350 figures on show, with frequent changes. The pinnacle of success has been reached when one's model is placed in Madame Tussaud's.

Modelling victims of the guillotine

The model of Madame Tussaud herself, eighty-one years old, and black bonneted, is still in the exhibition. This self-portrait was her last. Marie was born in Strasbourg, but brought up in Paris by an uncle, Philippe Curtius, a doctor who had his own wax exhibition. He taught Marie wax modelling, and she made her earliest surviving portrait, of Voltaire, when she was seventeen.

In 1780 Marie went to the Court of Versailles as tutor in wax modelling to Louis XVI's sister Elizabeth. So, when the Revolution broke out, she was imprisoned as a royalist, and only her skill in modelling saved her from the guillotine, the blade of which is now in the Chamber of Horrors, along with the death masks of Louis XVI and Marie Antoinette, which Marie was forced to make. Models of the nobility were needed by the Revolutionaries for propaganda, and the head of almost every distinguished victim was modelled either by Marie or her uncle.

After marrying (and leaving) Francois Tussaud, Marie came to England in 1802 with about thirty of her best models. For thirty-three years she toured the country with one of her sons, setting up her figures in halls and theatres, and making new models.

At last, in 1835, tired of travelling, Madame Tussaud opened her exhibition permanently in London.

The Tableaux

The tableaux are among the most popular of the exhibits, showing in all too life-like accuracy Guy Fawkes and the Gunpowder Plot and the execution of Mary, Queen of Scots in the hall of Fotheringhay Castle. But here too is the 'Sleeping Beauty' — in reality a portrait of Madame du Barry by Dr Curtius. It is the oldest figure in the exhibition.

Another great favourite among the tableaux is a reconstruction of the famous picture, by Victorian artist W. Yeames, of a small Royalist being interrogated by Cromwellians, called 'When Did You Last See Your Father?' Samuel Pepys is here, and the Brontë sisters posing for a portrait by their brother Branwell.

The Conservatory and Heroes

The Conservatory features portrait figures in wax of people in all walks of life, including Pele, the world famous footballer, Joan Collins, Liza Minelli and Arthur Scargill as well as the romantic novelist Barbara Cartland and Larry Hagman, portrayed as 'JR'. Among the superstars you will find Michael Jackson, David Bowie, and Daley Thompson.

These portrait figures are presented with sequences of changing lights and sounds.

The Grand Hall

The reigning sovereign has always been given a place of honour in the exhibition. Queen Elizabeth II (like all monarchs since George III) gave a sitting to the waxworks sculptor, and stands regally wearing evening dress. Prince Andrew was joined by the Duchess of York on their wedding day.

This magnificent hall is thronged with famous people — Queen Elizabeth and many other kings and queens of England, Shakespeare with Dickens and Sir Walter Scott; Sir Winston Churchill and Lloyd George; Pablo Picasso and Henry Moore, and Mrs Margaret Thatcher, the first woman to become a party leader and prime minister in Britain.

George Washington (modelled by Madame Tussaud) stands with other American presidents, including Abraham Lincoln and Ronald Reagan. Henry VIII is there with his six wives, and there is a group all modelled by Madame Tussaud — Voltaire, and Louis XVI, Marie Antoinette and their two young children, Madame Elizabeth and the Dauphin.

British politicians glare at one another, and Pope John Paul II smiles benignly.

The Chamber of Horrors

Far below the street the instruments of the death penalty lead to the sights and sounds of Victorian London and the omnipresence of Jack the Ripper. Murderers, executed for their crimes, are depicted in contemporary scenes. Nearby, present-day criminals are portrayed within the confines of prison punishment.

The Battle of Trafalgar

A hero of yesterday who has never lost appeal is Lord Nelson, and the spectacle of 'The Battle of Trafalgar . . . as it happened' draws great crowds, and is especially popular with boys.

The spectacle is dominated by the noise of cannon fire, sounding just as it did as Nelson's fleet approached the French and Spanish fleets. The battle is played out on an exact reproduction of the lower gun deck: guns, equipment, crew stripped for action amid the smoke and smell of battle, and above and around, in a sequence of light and sound, cannons fire, masts fall, ships collide and boarders are repulsed. (Recordings for the spectacle were made on the *Victory* at Portsmouth.)

After watching and listening to the battle, pass down to the orlop deck, below the waterline where Nelson is dying.

Admission
Open every day of the year except Christmas Day from 10 a.m. to 5.30 p.m. Admission charge.

Madame Tussaud's also runs the London Planetarium, which is next door, and you can buy a Combined Ticket.

For party bookings, contact the Party Booking Office, Madame Tussaud's and the London Planetarium, Marylebone Road, London, NW1. Telephone 01-486 1121 or 01-935 6861. Parties over 10 qualify for a reduction.

How to get there
As for the London Planetarium.

33. The London Planetarium

The London Planetarium star shows take place at regular intervals, so if you want to see both the stars and the waxworks, it may suit you to go into the Planetarium first. Here, under the green copper dome, you can study the universe of stars and planets, comets and galaxies with an astronomer a guide.

This man-made universe is produced by a complicated, massive almost creature-like £100,000 Zeiss projector. It contains some 29,000 separate parts of 200 optical projectors. It is 13 feet (4 m) high and weighs more than 2 tons. There are projectors for the Sun, the Moon, and the five 'naked-eye' planets—Mercury, Venus, Mars, Jupiter and Saturn — and between them two 'star carriers' project 8,900 stars, correctly spaced, correctly graduated in brightness.

At the beginning of this century, it was realised that a mechanical model of the heavens was impracticable. No model could be made to a workable scale. For instance if the sun were represented by a two-foot globe, the Earth (200 foot, 61 m, away) would be the size of a pea. The problem of reproducing the heavens was solved in 1918 by Dr Bauersfeld of the optical firm of Carl Zeiss, of Jena. But his instrument, remarkable as it was, showed only the stars in the Northern Hemisphere. Since that first machine, additions and technical improvements have been introduced, and the instrument in the London Planetarium incorporates all these. It was manufactured by the Zeiss company in West Germany and can show the position of the stars and planets as they appear from any place on earth, at any moment in time from fifty years before the birth of Christ to some two thousand years into the future. The programmes last about thirty minutes and are given between 11 a.m. and 4.30 p.m. In term time schools programmes are given at 11 a.m., Monday to Friday. There are also 'Laserium' shows on most evenings which combine laser effects and rock music. Further information is available by telephoning 01-486 2242.

Admission

The Planetarium is open all the year round (except Christmas Day), daily 11 a.m. to 4.30 p.m. Admission charge (also combined rate with Madame Tussaud's).

How to get there

Madame Tussaud's and the Planetarium are next door to one another in Marylebone Road. The easiest way to get there is to go to Baker Street station by Underground, or by one of the many buses passing nearby. Telephone 01-486 1121 for information.

Dickens lovers may like to cross the road after coming out of Madame Tussaud's. Just past the church of St Marylebone (where Robert and Elizabeth Browning were married) is Devonshire Terrace. Ferguson House, on the corner, replaces number 1 Devonshire Terrace, where Dickens lived from 1839 to 1851. While there he wrote several of his most famous books, including *The Old Curiosity Shop, Dombey and Son* and *David Copperfield*. By the entrance is a mural showing Dickens and some of his best known characters.

London's canals, which declined as industry switched to rail and road for transport, have been reviving in recent years as recreation areas. There are many pleasant walks along the towpaths (described in 'Discovering London's Canals' in this series) and there are trips along some stretches during the summer. At Little Venice (nearest Underground, Warwick Avenue), the junction of the Grand Union Canal and the Regent's Canal, Jason's Trip has its moorings (opposite 60 Blomfield Road W9). They run traditional narrow boats from Easter to October down to Camden Lock and back, a one and a half hour trip full of colour and movement along the Regent's Canal. Refreshment can be purchased on the boat and there is a craft shop at the moorings. For details of departure times, telephone 01-286 3428. Boats also operate from Port a Bella at Ladbroke Grove (Paddington Canal) and Camden Locks at Camden Town (Regent's Canal).

34. London's parks

Did you know that you can walk in parkland almost all the way from Trafalgar Square to Kensington Palace? Here is the route. Cross under Admiralty Arch, and skirt the Mall by walking along St James's Park towards Buckingham Palace. Then cross into Green Park, heading towards Hyde Park Corner. Cross into Hyde Park, and you can walk through its broad acres, and through Kensington Gardens right up to Kensington Palace.

For playing 'paille maille'

Most Londoners prefer the 93 acres (38 ha) of **St James's Park** to all others. It has a charming five-acre lake, pelicans, and is a sanctuary for migratory birds. There are fine views of Buckingham Palace and Whitehall too.

It was not laid out as a park until Charles II employed Le Notre, who had planned the gardens at Versailles. Le Notre drew up plans for a lake and islands, an aviary along Birdcage Walk, and a 600-yard (549 m) course where Charles and his favourites could play the old French game of *paille maille*.

No one plays *paille maille* here any more, but the game gave its name to Pall Mall.

A favourite place for duels

Green Park is still an informal park covering 53 acres (21 ha) and is beautiful all the year round, particularly in the spring, when crocuses and daffodils are out. It was once a favourite place for duels. As you walk through it look for the fardel rest in the Piccadilly pavement as you approach Hyde Park. This high bench was erected many years ago so that porters could rest their bundles, or fardels, there before toiling up the hill.

The traffic roars round Hyde Park Corner with such ferocity it is best to take the underpass and arrive in **Hyde Park** safely.

Wolves and hangings

Wolves once lived here and were such a menace to travellers they were ruthlessly hunted down by the Saxon kings. At one time the land belonged to the monks of Westminster Abbey, but at the Dissolution of the Monasteries Henry VIII enclosed the park and declared it royal property. He stocked it with deer, and he and his daughter Elizabeth hunted there.

Charles I opened the park to the public, and Cromwell reviewed his troops there. He had an undignified experience while driving a coach and six. The horses got out of control, and Cromwell was 'flung out of the coachbox upon the pole' and was carried along for some distance with his feet trailing on the ground. When Charles II was restored to the throne, Cromwell and other Parliamentarians who were buried in Westminster

Abbey were disinterred and hanged in ignominy at Tyburn. A plaque set into the road near Marble Arch marks the site of this terrible three-sided gallows. Numbers of people could be hanged at the same time, and a hanging was one of the most popular spectacles of the day, with hawkers selling gingerbread and generally making a holiday of the occasion.

Charles II made Hyde Park the centre of fashion, but by William III's reign it had become dangerous with footpads. When he went to live at Kensington Palace (because the country air was better for his asthma), he had Hyde Park hung with three hundred lamps to make his journeys safer. The lighted roadway that William used became known as La Route du Roi—the origin (probably) of Rotten Row.

The Serpentine, a lovely lake of 40 acres (16 ha), well-stocked with waterfowl, was made at the request of Queen Caroline, George II's wife. She created Kensington Gardens (where its share of the Serpentine is called the Long Water) by enclosing 300 acres (121 ha) of Hyde Park. She wanted to enclose that too, and St James's Park. But when she enquired the likely cost, Prime Minister Walpole replied severely: 'Three crowns, Madam—England, Scotland and Ireland!'

A notorious duel

In George III's reign Hyde Park became notorious for duelling, 172 duels being fought there during his reign. The most famous was between the bad Lord Mohun, and James Douglas, fourth Duke of Hamilton. Each man killed the other. In a letter telling of the duel, Dean Swift wrote: 'The dog Mohun was killed on the spot, but while the duke was over him, Mohun shortened his sword, and stabbed him in the shoulder to the heart. The duke died on the grass, before he could reach his house, and was brought home in his coach'.

A miscalculation

Marble Arch was designed by John Nash (died 1835), who also laid out Regent's Park. With the Marble Arch, however, he made a miscalculation. The original plan was to make the arch a spectacular main entrance to Buckingham Palace—but it was just a few inches too narrow for the state coach to go through. It was set up in Hyde Park in 1851.

Colourful occasions

Today Hyde Park covers 360 acres (146 ha) and is a place for picnics, for sleeping in the sun, or for listening to cranks and prophets at Speakers' Corner.

Royal Salutes (of forty-one guns) are fired in Hyde Park on special occasions such as the Queen's real birthday (21st April), her 'official' birthday (on a Saturday in June), the anniversary of her Accession (6th February), the Coronation anniversary (2nd June), the Duke of Edinburgh's birthday (10th June) and the Queen Mother's birthday (4th August).

Another big occasion for Hyde Park is the **Veteran Car Run,** held from Hyde Park to Brighton on the first Sunday in November. The veterans must have been manufactured between 1895 and 1904. The annual run is held in memory of the 'Emancipation Day' run to Brighton in November 1896 — to celebrate the lifting of the law which laid down that vehicles on a highway must not travel faster than 4 mph and must be preceded by a man walking ahead.

Peter Pan's garden

Kensington Palace was remodelled by Christopher Wren for William III in 1689—and till the death of George II in 1760 it was the official residence of the reigning monarch. Queen Victoria was born there in 1819—and lived there till her accession in 1837. Victoria was described as a child as 'a pretty little princess, plump as a partridge'—and she spent many hours playing in **Kensington Gardens,** which cover over 270 acres (109 ha). It is still a favourite park for children. First of all there is the statue of **Peter Pan,** near the Long Water. On the pedestal beneath him are fairies, rabbits and field mice, whose wings and ears have been polished over the years by the constant fondling of small caressing hands. The statue was erected in 1912.

Another favourite place in Kensington Gardens is the **Round Pond,** enjoyed equally by swans, dogs, children and adults. It is a great place for sailing boats or flying kites.

Leaving the Round Pond behind you, walk to the right up the Broad Walk. On the left, near Bayswater, there is a playground of see-saws and swings—and an **Elfin Oak,** now enclosed by a protective railing. It was carved in 1930 by Ivor Innes from an old stump from Richmond Park. The tree was restored in 1966 and a tiny plaque gives credit for the work to the fairies. (They had some help, however, from Spike Milligan, the actor.)

Tournaments and jousts

London's other great park is quite separate from St James's, Green Park, Hyde Park and Kensington Gardens. It is **Regent's Park,** roughly circular and covering 472 acres (191 ha). It includes the London Zoo. It was once one of the royal hunting parks and has always been well looked after. A mound was built round it in the early days to keep deer in and poachers out, and lodges were built for the gamekeepers, who were paid fourpence a day.

Regent's Park as we know it was laid out by Nash for the

Prince Regent. The favourite entrance is the Clarence Gate entrance from Baker Street, as it is so near transport and is the quickest way to the ducks.

Among the attractions of Regent's Park are the lake covering 22 acres (9 ha), where one can hire rowing boats, the rose garden (called Queen Mary's Garden as a tribute to her life-long interest in the park and its flower gardens) and the Open Air Theatre, where in the summer Shakespearean and other plays are performed.It is a magical setting for *A Midsummer Night's Dream,* though it is a good idea to take a rug: it can grow chilly, and the midges bite unprotected legs.

On Easter Monday the annual **London Harness Horse Parade** is held in the Inner Circle of Regent's Park. Judging takes place between 10 a.m. and noon.

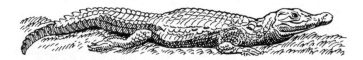

35. London Zoo

Choose a fine day (if you can) for your visit to London Zoo. Pack a lunch (although there are cafeterias and kiosks there) and set off *without* any food for the inhabitants. They are very adequately fed and to keep healthy they must keep to their diet. Besides, if animals learn to beg, they become so greedy that they will eat *anything* — coats, handbags, gloves — even cameras. They may also try to eat you.

The zoo's family usually numbers about eight thousand mammals, fish, reptiles, amphibians and birds. (No one bothers to count the insects.) It covers 36 acres (15 ha), with 'resident' quarters and the gardens. The magnificent lion terraces which were opened by the Queen in 1976 are a very popular attraction.

The most valuable and famous mammal in the zoo is Chia-Chia, the surviving giant panda of the pair presented to the British people by the Chinese Government in 1974. Chia-Chia (pronounced Cha-Cha) means 'Most Excellent'. There are few giant pandas in captivity and naturalists who know the jungles of China estimate that there are probably not more than 250 left in the wild. The most popular animals, the apes and the monkeys, are housed in the Michael Sobell Pavilions, where they live in family groups or as colonies. Visitors watch from covered walkways.

Elephants and rhinos have a large pavilion. The Snowdon Aviary, opened in 1965, is the zoo's first out of doors walk-through aviary. With its pools and waterfalls, it houses over 140 birds, including herons, egrets, ibises, toracos and spoonbills.

Housekeeping for the zoo family is expensive; it costs almost £250,000 a year. Some of the residents present food problems. The pink-feathered birds such as flamingoes and scarlet ibises can live on quite ordinary foods, but unless their diet includes pink chemicals called carotenoids they cannot grow pink feathers. To stop them turning white, these birds at London Zoo are given special foods which are rich in carotene pigments.

Finding enough ants for the ant-eaters would be difficult, but they thrive on a substitute diet of raw minced meat with milk and raw eggs. To keep reindeer in good condition, they need some of their natural food, a lichen called 'reindeer moss' which is specially imported.

One of the most delightful sections of the zoo is the 'moonlight world' in the basement of the Charles Clore Pavilion for Mammals. Here, day and night have been reversed so we can see nocturnal animals such as badgers going about their nightly activities. (Normally, during the day, they would be curled up and invisible in their sleeping boxes.)

Do not miss the Children's Zoo Farm, where you meet at close quarters all sorts of animals that make good pets, and where *small* children can have rides on tiny Shetland ponies or diminutive donkeys.

At certain times of the year children of any age can feel like explorers and ride a camel, donkey or pony or ride in a trap drawn by a llama. Children, adults and families can become Friends of the Zoo (for an annual subscription). They can visit London Zoo and Whipsnade Park every day except Christmas Day, take part in special events and receive regular newsletters. Write to the Membership Office, London Zoo, Regents Park, London NW1 4RY. For information about admission, opening and feeding times telephone 01-722 3333.

How to get there

London Zoo is a fair walk from Regent's Park underground station. Better to go to Baker Street station, and catch a number 74 bus which goes close to the Main Gate. (This bus comes from Knightsbridge, Hyde Park Corner and Marble Arch.) Alternatively, catch a number 3 or number 53 from Trafalgar Square, Piccadilly Circus or Regent Street. These buses will take you to Albany Street, within five minutes' walk of the Main or South Gates. Camden Town underground station is about ten minutes' walk away.

36. Polka Children's Theatre

Polka Children's Theatre in Wimbledon is a unique centre of child entertainment which goes by the motto 'Long live the theatre of magic and colour, music, craft, skill'. Established in 1967, it toured for twelve years until it found a home in a dilapidated building in south London, which, with the help of many donations, it has restored and equipped with numerous facilities for children.

The main attraction is the theatre itself which seats three hundred and is dedicated to Charlie Chaplin, 'The World's Greatest Clown'. It has been given an oriental decoration and presents plays, mimes performed in masks and puppet shows of all kinds — nearly all of the thirty-five shows in the repertoire mix actors and puppets to some degree.

Toys of Britain

Yet the Polka Theatre is also the headquarters of the British Toymakers' Guild and at the top of the main stairs an exhibition called 'Toys of Britain' has been set up. This includes fine examples of contemporary toys, some of which can be purchased from Mister Punch's Toyshop in the main exhibition hall. There is also an exhibition of Puppets of the World which houses the entire collection of Waldo and Muriel Lanchester, who from 1920 to 1955 were the main figures in British puppetry. Afternoon and holiday clubs in drama, mime, music and puppetry are open to a wide age range on a first come, first served basis through the Polka mailing list.

Adventure Room and Playground

Beyond the sphere of toys, workshops and shows, there are also rooms where children can entertain themselves: the Adventure Room and Playground provide a selection of worthwhile play apparatus and the Pantry is an entertainment in itself. The Pantry sells only home-made food and drinks, to be eaten in the compartments of a replica nineteenth-century train, as well as on cafe-styled tables under parasols or upstairs in the Link Gallery where birthday teas can be arranged.

Every sort of child is considered in the building and the aim is to avoid separating the handicapped from other children, so the building has been designed according to the needs of the disabled in order that they can participate in all the events on offer.

Admission

The building is open from Tuesday to Saturday. No admission charge. Telephone 01-543 4888 for information on the Theatre's performances.

How to get there
Polka is situated at 240 The Broadway in Wimbledon. South Wimbledon underground and Wimbledon main line stations are nearby.

37. The Musical Museum and Kew Bridge Steam Museum

The Musical Museum was founded in 1963 by Frank W. Holland MBE, in order to allow the public to hear automatic pianos, but the collection has now been extended to include self-playing instruments of all sorts. On them can be played any of the twenty thousand music rolls which the museum possesses, with players ranging from Rachmaninoff to Scott Joplin. Re-enacting pianos constitute the bulk of the exhibition, but you can also find pipe organs, musical boxes, dulcimers and even self-playing violins!

Admission
Open April to October inclusive on Saturdays and Sundays 2 p.m. to 5 p.m. Souvenirs, records and music rolls may be bought. Admission charge.

How to get there
The museum is in a church at 368 High Street, Brentford. Take the underground to Gunnersbury and then buses 237 or 267 which pass by the museum's door or 65 bus from South Ealing, Ealing Broadway or Richmond stations.

While you are in the area go and see the **Kew Bridge Steam Museum,** the world's biggest collection of large steam engines. These are awe-inspiring to see and were once described by L. T. C. Rolt as the 'most perfect expression of power'. Make sure especially to see the Grand Junction 90 inch (2286 mm) Cornish beam engine, which is the largest one working in the world. Made in 1845, it comes to life each weekend and is so big that 'Blue Peter' was once able to film a party *inside* the cylinder to celebrate its return to work. Traction engines and a railway engine are also on show.

Admission
The museum is open daily, 11 a.m. to 5 p.m. Engines are in steam at the weekends and on bank holiday Mondays. Free car park. Admission charge. For more details telephone 01-568 4757.

How to get there
Gunnersbury underground station is twenty minutes' walk away and main line trains go from Waterloo to Kew Bridge station and back every half hour.

38. The Cabinet War Rooms

Hidden 10 feet (3 metres) beneath the streets of Westminster is the now restored wartime headquarters of Winston Churchill. As you enter there is a display explaining the origins and purpose of the War Rooms, before you come to the complex itself. This comprises two parallel corridors, some 76 yards (70 metres) long, and the rooms off them. The first room is the Cabinet Room. Churchill's War Cabinet met here more than 100 times between May 1940 and May 1945. Among many items to look for are the red and green lamps, to indicate whether or not an air raid was in progress, and candles in case the power supply failed. Along the corridor are many of the original signs, indicating emergency water supplies and the weather above ground. (As a joke, during air raids the weather board was often marked 'Windy'!)

On the right is Churchill's private secretary's office, with 'Quiet Please' over the door. Further along the corridor, on the left, is the Transatlantic Telephone Room, from which Churchill could speak directly with President Roosevelt. Look at the heavy steel girders as you walk along the corridor: one, near a sealed door is marked 'Way out to Great George Street' — a reminder of where you are underground. Continue along the corridor and into the second corridor; you are now facing north. Here a display includes recordings of BBC broadcasts dating from the war and some of the radio equipment used by Churchill to make broadcasts from the War Rooms. Next come a series of offices. There are gas masks and steel helmets on the walls, while in General Ismay's office is a 'Most Secret' envelope. On the walls are fans — a reminder of how hot the rooms were without our modern air-conditioning. The Map Room is one of the largest and most impressive displays. Next to it is the 'Prime Minister's Room' (though Churchill slept here only three times during the Blitz). Nearby is a stack of rifles — ready for the last-ditch defence had Britain been invaded.

There is also a display of objects discovered when the rooms were being prepared for opening. It includes an antique 'Brown Bess' musket (no one knows how it got there) and an officer's sugar ration (three lumps), left behind when everyone left in 1945. On the way out is a souvenir shop.

Admission

The War Rooms are open every day, 10 a.m. to 5.50 p.m. and on Easter Monday, Spring Bank Holiday and Summer Bank Holiday. They are closed on New Year's Day, Good Friday, May Bank Holiday, Christmas Eve, Christmas Day and Boxing

Day. They may also be closed at short notice on State occasions. Admission charge.

How to get there

The nearest Underground station is Westminster. A large number of buses go nearby and any bus going to Parliament Square will take you there. The Cabinet War Rooms are next to the Government Offices in King Charles Street, which comes immediately before Downing Street if you walk from Parliament Square along Parliament Street towards Trafalgar Square. The entrance is next to Clive Steps — the steps from King Charles Street down to Horse Guards — and is well sign-posted.

39. The Imperial Collection

Based in Central Hall, Westminster, this collection is only two minutes' walk away from the Houses of Parliament. This is an impressive and colourful display of reproductions of crown jewels of the world. Using precious and semi-precious stones the collection is itself worth about £2 million. When not busy on one of his many official functions as London's Town Crier, Mr Peter Moore, may well be there to show you around. The collection is unique, many of the originals of the crown jewels it displays having been lost or destroyed in wars and revolutions. Such was the fate of the Russian, Persian, Bavarian, Prussian and French crowns.

The copies of the British Crown Jewels are more easily seen here than their originals at the Tower of London. Included in the display are the Coronation regalia and the Sovereign's Jewelled Sword, with which people are knighted.

There is a central display of Napoleon Bonaparte's crown jewels, while the Austrian display includes the crown of the Prince of Transylvania. Other ill-fated royal familes are represented: there is the ruby and diamond tiara of Marie Antoinette and the Russian crown jewels. There is also a display of famous diamonds, including the Cullinan — the largest in the world — and some which have brought misfortune to their owners. For further information telephone 01-222 0770.

Admission

The exhibition is open every day except Sunday from 10 a.m. to 6 p.m. from March to October and from 11 a.m. to 5 p.m. from November to February. Admission charge, with reductions for parties of children in groups of twenty or more.

How to get there

St James's Park and Westminster Underground stations are only a couple of minutes' walk away, or take any bus going to Parliament Square or Westminster Abbey. From Parliament

Square walk along the right hand side of Broad Sanctuary, away from the Houses of Parliament. Central Hall is immediately in front of you, though to get to the exhibition you must go to the other side of the hall, to the Matthew Parker Street entrance.

40. The Museum of Mankind

Although it is the Ethnography Department of the British Museum, the Museum of Mankind is a separate museum, based in Burlington Gardens, between New Bond Street and Regent Street and behind the Royal Academy. It holds exhibitions illustrating overseas societies and cultures. They depict the way of life of particular peoples and the regularly-changing exhibitions cover cultures from many places around the world. Film shows are given from Tuesdays to Fridays in the Film Theatre (with seating for 69 people). Special shows can be booked (though notice must be given) and parties of 10 or more must also book in advance. Videos are also shown, in the Schools Room (which can seat 29 people). Films such as *The Hazda* about a Tanzanian hunting people, *Trobriand Cricket* about how the islanders of Papua New Guinea play cricket and *Manioc Bread* about how American Indians make bread from the poisonous manioc root, are some of many available.

Children's Worksheets are available from the Information Desk and the main exhibitions also have teachers' notes. Some recent exhibitions have included those on the North American Indians, Madagascar and special pieces in the Ethnographic Collection. During the school holidays there are special events for children with activities based on current exhibitions. For full information about current exhibitions and booking for films and videos, telephone 01-437 2224, extension 43.

Admission

The Museum is open from Monday to Saturday, 10 a.m. to 5 p.m., Sundays 2.30 p.m. to 6 p.m. It is closed during Christmas, on Good Friday and on the first Monday in May. Admission free.

How to get there

Piccadilly Circus and Green Park Underground stations are both only a few minutes' walk away. A large number of buses run nearby and the Museum is best reached by walking through Burlington Arcade from Piccadilly.

41. The Guinness World of Records

In Shaftesbury Avenue is a modern development, the 'Trocadero' complex. Go inside and up the escalator and you come to the Guinness World of Records exhibition. As you go in you are met by a model of the world's tallest man, Robert Wadlow, who grew to a height of 8 feet 11.1 inches (2.72 metres). You can shake his hand, compare your height with his and watch a short film about him. Next to him, on a table, is a model of the world's smallest woman.

Immediately opposite is a model of the world's heaviest man, who weighed 1,070 lb (485 kg)! He is on a large weighing machine, so a group of you can measure your combined weight against his — though it's doubtful that you'll equal it! Nearby is an electronic display, which is always working, showing the population of the world, of the United Kingdom and of China. In the next room are displays including buttons to be pressed for sound effects and information about record-breaking sneezes, snores, hiccoughs and yawns.

You then go upstairs, past a revolving display of some record-breaking men and women, including the most-tattooed lady and the man with the strongest teeth, and come to a number of television sets showing records actually being set — such as the longest domino tumbling and the highest shallow dive into water. Walk through the jaw bone of a blue whale to a section on animal record-breakers. There is information about cats, rabbits and the largest surviving litter of puppies as well as spiders, scorpions and snake skins. Next is a display of space records — satellites, walks in space and the like — followed by more earth-bound engineering records. There are numerous electronic displays with buttons to press for information on subjects ranging from the longest bridges and tunnels to records of the natural world, including Mount Everest, the Grand Canyon and the hottest, driest and even windiest places on Earth. In the sports display are models showing the heights for record pole vaults and high jump and the distance for the long jump, as well as film of sportsmen and women in action. Again, computer displays will give you the most up-to-date information on sporting records.

Downstairs again is a display including a juke box which will play record-breaking pop-tunes. There are displays of film and stage records as well as many others from the world of entertainment, and a real cinema projector which you can 'control'. There is an excellent souvenir shop as you go out.

Admission
The Guinness World of Records is open every day, except

97

Christmas Day, from 10 a.m. to 10 p.m. Last admissions 9 p.m. Admission charge, with reductions for children and adults in parties of ten or more. If you need further details, telephone 01-439 7331.

How to get there

Trocadero is on the north side of Shaftesbury Avenue. Come out of the Piccadilly Circus Underground Station on the Shaftesbury Avenue side (subway 5) and the building is only a minute's walk away; or take any bus to Piccadilly Circus.

42. The Cricket Memorial Gallery

This is the main cricket museum in England and naturally is based at Lord's Cricket Ground. The collection was begun in 1865 when advertisements in the national newspapers asked for gifts of cricket bygones to form a cricket museum. In 1953 the Collection moved from the Member's Pavilion to a separate building, built as a memorial to the cricketers who died in the World Wars — hence the name 'Memorial Gallery'. Here you can see pictures, engravings and photographs of the history of cricket. These include some very rare and fine pictures, of cricket being played in Italy, on the first Lord's Cricket Ground and even an early eighteenth-century match being played in the USA. Less obvious, perhaps, are collections of old cigarette cards recording the players of the past, such as Tate and Duckworth, Quaife and Flowers.

W. G. Grace is, of course, remembered here in many forms. His snuff box, short notes by him, and his highly colourful belt are all here as well as many pictures. Also on display are the Ashes. Fortunately for English cricket enthusiasts these do not actually go to Australia when that country wins them, but remain at Lord's all the time. You can also see how the cricket bat developed into its present form, from the curiously curved and very heavy bats of the past — which look more like the war clubs of a ferocious tribe than implements of the 'summer game'.

If you are a cricket enthusiast already then you will find almost everything here of great interest, while for others it provides a glimpse of the history of the game. For real students of cricket there is also the Library while, for those who regard going to Lord's as a pilgrimage, you can, outside the cricket season, arrange to visit the Long Room.

Admission

The Memorial Gallery is open on match days from Monday to Saturday, 10.30 a.m. to 5 p.m. Outside the cricket season, by prior arrangement with the Curator, Mondays to Fridays, 10 a.m. to 5 p.m. Admission charge. The Library is open at the same times and can be used, free of charge, by appointment with the Curator. Visits to the Long Room can be made during the off season, by appointment with the Curator. Telephone 01-289 1611.

How to get there

St John's Wood Underground station is close at hand, and the Ground is a short walk along Wellington Road. There are buses from Baker Street to Lord's.

TELECOM TECHNOLOGY SHOWCASE

Just round the corner from St Paul's Cathedral is Telecom Technology Showcase, where you can find out all about telecommunications. Starting with the pioneers of telegraphy, the exhibition tells the story of how telecommunications have developed over the past 150 years or so and how they are likely to develop in the future. It is not so very long since few telephones had dials and all calls were connected by operators (there is a reconstruction of an old exchange switchboard) but now some telephones with built-in microprocessors can 'think'.

As you would expect, you can operate many of the displays to find out how they work. There is a working Prestel set you can use, for example, and a Strowger telephone exchange where you can see the call you are making pass through. An elaborate telephone owned by the Rothschilds about 1900 and black 'candlestick' phones contrast oddly with slim, press-button modern fittings, but one item which has changed very little until recently is the telephone kiosk. The 'Jubilee' box of 1936 is still most people's idea of what a kiosk should look like.

The Showcase is at 135 Queen Victoria Street, next to the Mermaid Theatre. Telephone: 01-248 7444. It is open Monday to Friday, 10 a.m. to 5 p.m. and closed on bank holidays. Admission is free. Blackfriars is the station for British Rail and for Circle and District lines on the Underground. There are many buses including 6, 9, 11 and 15. Go to Ludgate Circus and walk down New Bridge Street.

43. North Woolwich Old Station Museum

The Great Eastern Railway from Stratford to the river Thames reached the North Woolwich terminus in 1847. The wooden station put up then was replaced in 1854 by the present building, that now houses the Museum of the Great Eastern Railway, overlooking the river and the Woolwich Ferry.

As you enter the booking hall you are greeted by staff wearing the long tail coats worn by railway officials in the 1920s and the booking office where you would have bought your tickets is furnished with furniture and equipment of the same period. By the fire there is an enormous kettle which suggest the railwaymen were great tea drinkers! On the walls there are name and number plates from the locomotives which used to steam in and out of the station. Display cases and photographs tell the history of the railway and the people who ran it.

In the turntable pit outside stands the oldest GER locomotive, number 229, and in the platform area there is a Peckett industrial tank locomotive which is steamed on some Sundays in summer.

Admission
The station is open Monday to Saturday 10 a.m. to 5 p.m., Sundays and bank holidays 2 a.m. to 5 p.m. The Museum is closed Christmas Day and Boxing Day. No admission charge. Telephone: 01-474 7244.

How to get there
The North London Link Line, Richmond to North Woolwich. Buses 58, 69, 101 and 278 pass the door; alight at the stop for the ferry. The river can be crossed by the ferry or the adjacent foot tunnel. Frequent buses run between Woolwich or Greenwich and the Thames Barrier: 51, 96, 177 and 180.

44. The Rotunda, Museum of Artillery

The Museum of Artillery in the Rotunda, at Woolwich, is unusual because both the exhibits and the building that houses them were brought here to form the museum. The collection was begun in 1778 by Captain (later Lieutenant-General) Sir William Congreve to instruct artillery officers; and a Repository was built for it in what became the Royal Arsenal. In 1805 the building and most of the collection was destroyed by fire but in 1819 it moved to its present site when Colonel Sir William Congreve (the founder's son) arranged for the re-erection there of the 'Rotunda'. This had originally been one of six temporary 'tents' designed by John Nash, in 1814, for the allied sovereigns to meet in Carlton House Gardens (now St James's Park). Moved to

Woolwich, it was given a permanent roof and a central supporting pillar and has remained there ever since. The museum holds a collection of guns dating from the fourteenth century, which allows you to follow the development of artillery from the earliest times to the modern day.

One of the oldest pieces in existence is kept here, a 'Bombard' which could fire a stone ball weighing 160 lbs (72.5 kg), as well as some of the earliest machine guns. Also on display are some of Congreve's famous Rockets — used during the Napoleonic Wars — as well as another of his inventions, 'Congreve's Perpetual Motion Clock'. There are leather guns and a Burmese cannon — cast in the form of a dragon — which was captured during the 1885 Burmese War.

Here also you can see the different types of muzzle-loading and breech-loading guns, how 'rifling' works and the difference between forged and cast guns. In another display is the gun carriage which carried Queen Victoria's coffin, and the carriage which carried both Edward VII and George V. Here too is the 'Nery Gun' from the First World War. For their gallant action on 1st September 1914 three members of this gun's team won the Victoria Cross. Altogether there are hundreds of exhibits, with many displayed outside as well as in the Rotunda. For further information, telephone 01-856 5533, extension 385.

Admission

The Museum is open every day of the year, except for Christmas Eve, Christmas Day, Boxing Day, New Year's Day and Good Friday, from mid-day on Mondays to Fridays and from 1 p.m. at weekends. From April to October it closes at 5 p.m. and from November to March closing time is at 4 p.m. Admission is free.

How to get there

The Rotunda is just off Repository Road in Woolwich — opposite the Royal Artillery Barracks. Woolwich Dockyard and Woolwich Arsenal British Rail stations are nearby. Numbers 53, 54, 75 and 122A buses go to the Rotunda, or you could take a river boat to the Thames Barrier which is only a little further away than the railway stations.

A useful telephone number to know is that of the London Tourist Board, 26 Grosvenor Gardens, London SW1 — 01-730 3488.

The publishers have made every effort to ensure the accuracy of the information in this book, but times of opening in particular are liable to alteration and intending visitors are advised to check with the London Tourist Board before setting out.

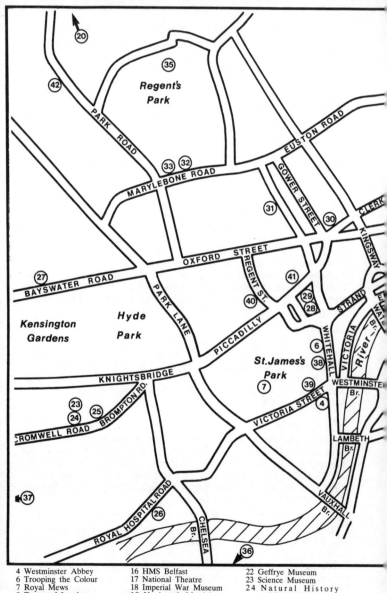

4 Westminster Abbey	16 HMS Belfast	22 Geffrye Museum
6 Trooping the Colour	17 National Theatre	23 Science Museum
7 Royal Mews	18 Imperial War Museum	24 Natural History Museum
8 Tower of London	19 National Maritime Museum	25 Victoria and Albert Museum
9 Tower Bridge	20 Royal Air Force Museum	26 National Army Museum
12 Monument	21 Bethnal Green Museum of Childhood	27 London Toy and Model Museum
13 St Paul's Cathedral		
14 Museum of London		
15 London Dungeon		

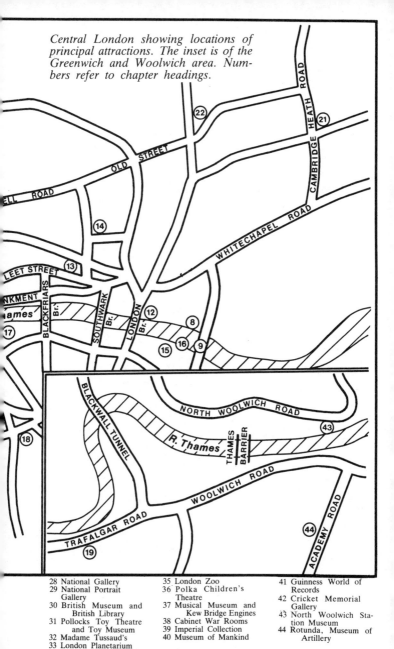

Central London showing locations of principal attractions. The inset is of the Greenwich and Woolwich area. Numbers refer to chapter headings.

INDEX

Printed in Great Britain by C. I. Thomas & Sons (Haverfordwest) Ltd,
Press Buildings, Merlins Bridge, Haverfordwest.